GLASGOW'S AIRPORT

DUGALD CAMERON

Cover Painting by Dugald Cameron

AUTUMN 1934 AT RENFREW

On the ground are: a Fox Moth of SMT; D.H.86s of Railway Air Services and Imperial Airways; Dragon of Midland & Scottish Air Ferries. In the hangar is the former Hillman's Airways aircraft which was sold to Aberdeen Airways whose Scion G-ACUV can just be seen.

In the air are: Highland Airways' General Aircraft Monospar; two de Havilland Moths, belonging to Archie Fraser and the Scottish Flying Club and Midland & Scottish's Airspeed Ferry.

G-ACEJ D.H.83 Fox Moth — Scottish Motor Traction; G-ACAN D.H.84 Dragon — Aberdeen Airways (in Hillman's livery)
G-ACVY D.H.86 'Mercury' — Railway Air Services; G-ACPL D.H.86B 'Delphinus' — Imperial Airways
G-ACDL D.H.84 Dragon — Midland & Scottish Air Ferries; G-ACUV Short Scion 1 — Aberdeen Airways
G-ACEW General Aircraft ST4 Monospar Inverness — Highland Airways; G-ACGD D.H.60 G-111 Moth — Archibald Fraser
G-ABZV D.H.60 G-111 Moth — Scottish Flying Club; G-ACBT Airspeed Ferry — Midland & Scottish Air Ferries

HOLMES McDOUGALL LTD • EDINBURGH & GLASGOW

BIBLIOGRAPHY

Aviation in Scotland	J.D. Gillies and J.L. Wood, Royal Aeronautical Society, Glasgow Branch.
Zero 8 to M8	J.D. Gillies paper presented to Royal Aeronautical Society, Glasgow.
Action Stations	David J. Smith, Patrick Stephens Ltd.
Sword in the Sky	Peter V. Clegg.
British Independent Airlines	Tony Merton Jones, LAAS/Merseyside Aviation Enthusiasts' Society.
The Story of Loganair	Iain Hutchison, Western Isles Publishing Co. Ltd.
Glasgow's Own (History of 602 Squadron)	Dugald Cameron, Squadron Prints

ISBN 0 7157 2841-5

© Dugald Cameron 1990

Printed and published by Holmes McDougall Ltd., Allander House, 137-141 Leith Walk, Edinburgh EH6 8NS.
Tel: 031-554 9444. Fax: 031-554 4051.

Designed by James W. Murray.

Typeset by Trinity Typesetting, Edinburgh. 031-553 6903.

ACKNOWLEDGEMENTS

I am grateful to the following friends and acquaintances for their generous help and assistance, and in many cases, the use of their photographs. Every effort has been made to find all copyright owners, any omissions will be rectified at the first opportunity.

Walter M. Bell   for both his reminiscences and access to his photographic collection.
Alan Carlaw   as usual, for his patient support and personal contribution on the history of Abbotsinch and the new Glasgow Airport.
Peter V. Clegg   for most generous access to his own material and publications on the Scottish pioneer aviators.
Philip Jarrett   for his contribution on the Beardmore Flying School.
Winifred Orchard   for her kindness and assistance in the face of
(nee Drinkwater)   great personal difficulty.
George C. Pinkerton   for his unfailing courtesy and personal reminiscences of the early days, 602 Squadron and the Scottish Flying Club.
John Stroud   without whose generosity in making available his records and photographs, the book could not have been produced.

J. Becket	David Shepherd
T.K. Black	Ray Sturtivant
W.R. Chorley	Allan Topp
Ian Crosbie	R.A.R. Wilson
Ian Johnston	Viscount Weir
John King	Wilf G. White
Jimmy Logan	
Gordon McAdie	together with
Tom McFadyen	
Alex. McGregor	Minute books of the *Scottish Flying Club.*
C. Hector MacLean	Minutes of *Renfrew Town Council* and its committees.
Alex. Morrison	Archives of the *University of Glasgow.*
Charles Oakley	The Editor of the *Glasgow Herald.*
Alan J. Reid	The local History Library at Paisley.
Gordon Reid	Scottish Air News.
R.G. Rosenbloom	Central Scotland Aviation Group.
	Scottish Airports Limited

Pionair, G-AHCU, 'Charles Ulm' landing over the Hillington Road, early 1960s.

Viscount of Icelandair taking-off from Renfrew, early 1960s.

A Scandanavian Airlines System Caravelle, on the approach to Glasgow Airport. The shipyard cranes of John Brown's form the backdrop.

This book is intended to illustrate the history of Glasgow's two airports, particularly that of the first, Renfrew, which occupied a central role in the early development of civil aviation in Scotland and can trace its origins to before the First World War, when powered flight was in its infancy. The second, built nearby at Abbotsinch and, like Renfrew, originally a military airfield, has become the major player in Scotland's civil aviation arena. However, Prestwick Airport was once scheduled to take over Renfrew's role. A good account of the political history of this debate is given in W.J. McKechin's 'Tale of Two Airports'. The arguments over where and what should be Glasgow's airport comes complete with an extensive catalogue of lost opportunities.

The Royal Burgh of Renfrew on the south bank of the River Clyde, adjacent to both the City of Glasgow to the East and its fellow Royal Burgh, Paisley to the South, has numerous claims to fame. Yet mention its name and many people around Glasgow will still think of the Renfrew Ferry — an institution which until 1984 conveyed passengers and vehicles over the Clyde between Renfrew and Yoker, one of a number on the upper Clyde, all of which except the Renfrew Ferry, have been made redundant by the new tunnel and bridges. A ferry at Renfrew still crosses the river though in much reduced circumstances, providing only a passenger service. Like her erstwhile sister, the Govan Ferry, the old ferries were the stuff of tale and legend. Fond memories of many trips on the steam ferry, after the Second World War, bring back the irresistible aroma of hot steam and oil, and the visual delights of her reciprocating machinery, including the pulley and chain which actually drove and guided her.

Further delights awaited on both sides of the river in the presence of Italian Cafes, the one on the Renfrew shore being the famous Coia's, where, amidst its marbled splendour and entrancing aroma, hot peas and a whole range of Italian ice-cream delicacies tempted juvenile and adult palates alike. The North bank could also boast its own Ferry Café and, on the way to the ferry, one of the smelliest public toilets in the West of Scotland! No matter how genteel one might be, it was never a 'loo'! Just at Coia's Café was the tram terminus, from which a short ride would take you near the Airport, and further on to Paisley or even exotic Speirsbridge. The Glasgow tramway system was itself an art form which none the less provided a magnificent and much loved public utility, unmatched since its sad demise in 1962. From 1943, until February, 1957, what had become the number 28 tram, terminated at Speirsbridge, just short of Rouken Glen, less than half the original distance.

A visit to Renfrew Airport with a trip on the ferry was a wee adventure then and the close view of the many ocean going ships on their way to and from the Glasgow docks, a common pleasure. Like the steam ferry, the trade which made the Clyde is gone and the salmon are returning. The great arts of manufacture on Clydeside were carelessly abandoned and the new products which must replace the locomotives, ships and heavy engineering, are only slowly beginning to appear — too often, they are but echoes of much nobler music. The City of Glasgow celebrated its status as European City of Culture in 1990. Its native culture, however, was based on making things, yet those so engaged rarely saw that what they were making — the great ships and locomotives — were themselves as much 'art' as the painting and sculpture, which they so often imported from abroad.

I am grateful to my many friends and acquaintances in the aviation enthusiast world for their generosity and patience in assisting me with this book. Without the unstinting help and encouragement of John Stroud, doyen of air transport writers, it would never have come to any sort of conclusion. From his, and his wife Pat's personal experiences and amazing archives, I have been able to draw on unrivalled material and I dedicate my modest effort to them both.

To my old friends, David Reid of Ayr, who has kindled the fire of aviation enthusiasm in so many ways, whilst at the same time nobly fighting in Prestwick's corner, and to Wilf White, veteran aviation photographer, may I offer my thanks for their friendship. To Walter Bell, Philip Jarrett and Peter Clegg, I am indebted for their generous and vital assistance. Alan Carlaw, my colleague in Squadron Prints has, as always, been the model of patience and timely assistance, as have my colleagues at Glasgow School of Art, James Murray, Maria Walsh, Jeanette Scott and George Rawson.

My thanks also go to Frank Baillie, Chief Executive of Holmes McDougall, for providing the impetus and opportunity to publish this book and to Edwin Ketley for his courtesy and company during the production.

CONTENTS

Renfrew aerodrome around 1928/29. In front of the rear hangars are Beardmore's Flying School's Bristol Type 89s and Avro 504s. On the right is the Imperial Airways Armstrong Whitworth Argosy I G-EBLF 'City of Glasgow'. In the foreground is an Avro 504 and a Fairey Fawn of 602 Squadron.

RENFREW, Cradle of Scotland's Aviation.

TRAVELLERS using the M8 motorway, to the west of the City of Glasgow, will detect few signs of the history which lies below their wheels. Nothing on that section of the M8 between the Hillington and Glasgow Airport slip roads shows that it once contained part of the old Renfrew Airport. Indeed, that its main runway, coincidentally designated 08/26 from its compass headings, lay near to the site on which the new motorway was built.

Those with some knowledge of the local history of Renfrew will recognise the enduring presence of Arkleston Cemetery and the line of Black Poplar trees which provided Renfrew Airport with a unique landmark, causing the late C.G. Grey founder and editor of 'The Aeroplane' to comment on the curiosities of the Scots' sense of humour which sited an aerodrome next to a cemetery! Renfrew Airport was always too small — even for the early aeroplanes and before much of the building took place around it. It was substantially expanded during World War II but was still too small. However Renfrew Airport occupies a particular and significant place in the history of British aviation as well as a central role in that of Scotland.

The pioneers in any kind of human activity are often beaten by time, being usually just too far ahead for commercial success. It's intriguing to dream of what might have been and how the West of Scotland might have played an even greater role in aircraft design and production had not Beardmore's been so over extended that they had to close their aviation division at Dalmuir in 1924. They were unique, among the aircraft producers on Clydeside during World War I, in having a true design capability. Of course, they might just have been beaten by the enthusiasts of the Scottish Aviation Company at Barrhead or the Lanark School of Aviation, both founded in 1911. They were no doubt inspired by the stirring events at Lanark Race Course during Scotland's first flying meeting there in August of the previous year. Two months before on 2nd, 3rd and 4th June 1910, one of the performers, James Radley, had demonstrated his Blériot type aircraft in the grounds of Pollok House, giving Glasgow and the West of Scotland its first public demonstration of powered flight. The 'Daily Mail' round-Britain air-race in 1911, with Lord Northcliffe offering a prize of £10,000, included a stop at Paisley, using the old racecourse on Greenock Road. Among the competitors was the flamboyant, pioneer aviator, Colonel S.F. Cody. He reached Paisley on 29th July, "attired in lounge suit, gloves and soft hat. His doggedness won him great admiration". This was the first time aeroplanes had been seen in Paisley, and some spectators were out as early as 4.30 a.m.! The venue for this, Paisley's earliest taste of flying, was but a mile or so from today's Glasgow Airport.

Lanark Aviation Meeting, 6th - 13th
August, 1910. Radley allotted No.13,
changed it to 131.
James Radley, first public demonstration
of flying in Glasgow at Pollok Park, 2nd,
3rd, 4th June 1990.

The accident of Renfrew's choice as a flying field for military purposes was typical, as so many airports had their origins this way. Some of our present problems indeed may be traced back to these somewhat ad-hoc decisions, though the availability of land suitable for flying purposes, is rarely plentiful and certainly wasn't around Glasgow.

It is also interesting to note that neither of Glasgow's airports has lain within the City's boundaries and thus its full control. Renfrew fell within and belonged to the Royal Burgh of Renfrew and Abbotsinch, though in 1966 belonging to the then Glasgow Corporation, came under Renfrew County Council for planning purposes being just North of Paisley Burgh boundary. With the Local Government reorganisation of 1975, Glasgow Airport came within the Renfrew District of Strathclyde Region.

There is also some irony in the origins of the long and weary argument about where the airport for Glasgow should be sited. It was the great David McIntyre of 602 (City of Glasgow) Squadron Auxiliary Air Force who had much to do with both the selection of Abbotsinch, as a more suitable place than Renfrew for the operating of his Squadron, *and*, the development of Prestwick as an airport and as an industrial base, for the development of his company, Scottish Aviation Ltd. Indeed, McIntyre, whilst Flight Commander of 602, planned the new Prestwick Airport at Skiff Cottage in the grounds of fellow pilot Denis McNab's house at Howood. Sadly his vision of Prestwick as a great international aviation centre has never been widely shared by those in places of political and commercial power.

Undoubtedly, Abbotsinch's proximity to the City of Glasgow has proven to be attractive to travellers, if not to those living under its flight paths. This too

Inauguration of British Airways' Super Shuttle, 30th August, 1983. Three Concordes at Glasgow.

was Renfrew's original bonus point, though its restricted size, and inability to be properly expanded to suit increasing operational requirements, finally killed it. After a somewhat protracted debate, its services were transferred a mile and a half away west to the former RAF and RN aerodrome at Abbotsinch. Prestwick was the Government of the day's original choice, however Glasgow interests prevailed upon the Macmillan Government and even though the City's Corporation was initially reluctant to take on the new Airport, an attractive financial proposition to them by the Government settled the matter and Renfrew, cradle of Scotland's aviation gave way to Glasgow Airport, at Abbotsinch, on 2nd May, 1966.

The brooding presence of Arkleston Cemetery and its cheerier neighbour, Arkleston Farm, have looked down upon a remarkable aeronautical kaleidoscope during this century — a history of aviation stretching from James Weir's early experiments before the First World War and the rudimentary biplanes of that calamity through the de Havilland Moths, Dragons and Dragon Rapides of the inter-war years; joined by large numbers of American fighter and bomber aircraft shipped to and from the Clyde during the Second World War, to the post war period of DC-3s, Vikings, Viscounts, Vanguards; and at the end of Renfrew's life, the jet airliner in the shape of the BAC One-Eleven. The jet age had, of course, arrived earlier with the re-equipping of 602 Squadron at Renfrew, temporarily transferred from Abbotsinch, with de Havilland Vampires and Gloster Meteors.

Renfrew was well known for being a friendly airport, as if to compensate for its restricted size and often lousy weather. Like Scottish flying in general, it never-the-less had an excellent safety record, particularly meritorious in view of both the climate and the topography, and in the early days, the complete lack of flying aids. These early pioneers were canny fliers and careful in the choice and maintenance of their aircraft. Their exemplary operational record testifies to their skill. That the routes they pioneered, including the first from Renfrew, are still in operation by British Airways and Loganair testifies to their vision.

Since little physically remains to remind us of Renfrew and its part in the history of aviation, there must be gratitude to those who perpetuated its memory in some of the street names used in the new housing estate built off Sandy and Newmains Roads, among which are, Viking and Vanguard Ways, Viscount Avenue, and though it never flew from Renfrew, Trident Way.

Abbotsinch, or Glasgow Airport as it is now known, was first used for flying in 1933. During the previous year it had been surveyed and developed to accommodate No.602 (City of Glasgow) Squadron of the Auxiliary Air Force who were then based nearby at Renfrew. The Squadron moved in January, 1933, with their Westland Wapiti aircraft. A variety of other RAF units used the base prior to 602 moving to the east of Scotland at the outbreak of World War II after which the Station became host to a number of different units, many of which however, were connected with maritime operations. It was not surprising therefore that on 11 August, 1943, the Station was transferred to the control of the Royal Navy and HMS *Sanderling*, as it became known, was commissioned on 20 September that year. In Fleet Air Arm use, it served as an aircraft maintenance yard and was home to a number of FAA squadrons. 602 Squadron reformed there after the war with Spitfires and 1830 with 1843 Squadron RNVR of the Scottish Air Division were also based together with 1967 Flight from 666 A.O.P. Squadron.

The development of aviation in the 1950s was indeed considerable. Bigger and faster aircraft were being introduced to cope with passenger and cargo flights and it was realised that Renfrew had been extended to its limit and a new airport for Glasgow had to be found. The Fleet Air Arm at Abbotsinch had diminished considerably and it was closed on 31 October, 1963, and the airfield passed to the Ministry of Transport and Civil Aviation for development of the site as the new Glasgow Airport. Much work, however, was necessary to convert this military site for use as a civil airport and it took almost three years for this work to be completed. The transfer of services from Renfrew took place on 2 May, 1966.

When opened, the new terminal building seemed large enough for the airport's forseeable needs of air passengers but during the past 25 years it has been developed and extended on a number of occasions and in 1990 underwent considerable extension to virtually double the size of the main building.

The twentieth century has witnessed Man's love affair with aviation, from Kitty Hawk to Concorde, and into space. It has seen the realisation of a dream which must have existed from the dawn of history and witnessed its use in the most dismal of human affairs, and the most sublime — the eternal human dilemma. Pride can be taken in Scotland's place in this adventure and in Glasgow's particular contribution.

T H E   E A R L Y   D A Y S

WHAT might have been often provides a tantalising contrast to what really did happen. Had Percy Pilcher, sometime lecturer in Naval Architecture at Glasgow University, not killed himself in 1899, he might have just beaten the Wright brothers and been the first to fly a heavier-than-air, powered aircraft. Barrhead and Lanark might have featured as centres of flying training; Dalmuir and Inchinnan could have been major locations for aircraft design and manufacture; and Cathcart, the focus for the development of the autogyro and helicopter. However, aviation did not replace or even supplement shipbuilding on the Clyde. The collapse of the market for military aircraft and the generally difficult economic conditions after the First World War, caused Beardmore's to close its aviation division at Dalmuir in 1921 though it was re-opened in 1924 for design and manufacture, and enjoyed some success before finally it closed in 1929. The associated story of Beardmore's Renfrew Flying School, is one which stands on its own.

During the later years of its existence, frustrated travellers often asked how Renfrew Airport came into being — the present Lord Weir was one and in answer, was told that his great uncle James was the man responsible. James G. Weir, brother of the first Lord Weir, was among the first licence holders from the Royal Aero Club, No. 24 dated 8th November 1910, and had been conducting flying experiments thereafter — from fields in the Moorpark area of Renfrew, as they were probably the most convenient flat area in the locality. It was here that, one day just before the outbreak of the First World War, Capt. A.C.H. MacLean, 'landings officer' of his Royal Flying Corps. Squadron was out for a drive. Looking over a hedge, he chanced upon 'Young Weir' at his experiments and decided that, on that basis, it must be a good enough site for a flying field — and so, it would seem, the area of land between the Newmains Farm and Arkleston Cemetery became designated for future flying activities. The outbreak of war in August 1914, provided the dismal catalyst for its eventual establishment as a military airfield.

William Douglas Weir, created first Viscount Weir of Eastwood in 1938, was born into the family engineering firm of G. & J. Weir Ltd., Holm Foundry, Cathcart. He left the High School of Glasgow at the age of 16 to enter the firm, moving progressively to the top. His organisational talents were recognised by the Lloyd George Government of 1915, when he was appointed Director of Munitions, Scotland, in the newly created Ministry of Munitions, and later Director of Aeronautical Supplies. He was to play an influential part in the creation of the independent Royal Air Force, on 1st April, 1918, persuading a reluctant General Trenchard to become its first chief. Another Glaswegian significantly involved in the birth of an independent air force was the Royal Flying Corps.' Lt. General Sir David Henderson. Weir's abilities continued to be employed by Government and indeed he was Air Minister in the late 1930s. Weirs, were among the first Clydeside engineering firms to be awarded contracts for the construction of aircraft and engines during the First World War under the great expansion scheme of 1915.

James G. Weir was an early flying enthusiast, much to the chagrin of his brother, William. After service with the Royal Flying Corps. during the War and reaching the rank of Brigadier, (converted to Air Commodore in RAF days), he took a serious interest in Juan de la Cierva's development of the Autogiro. Indeed G. & J. Weir became a licensee of the Cierva Co. and, in the period up to the outbreak of the Second World War, Weirs developed a number of Autogiros and indeed a helicopter. The imperatives of the 1939-45 conflict brought these developments to a premature end, though James Weir remained Chairman of the Cierva Company well into the 1960s. At one time, he commuted by Autogiro between his home at Dalrymple, Ayrshire, and the works at Cathcart, using the Weir recreation ground as a landing field! He also owned the D.H.51 G-EBIQ, based at Renfrew and used by the Scottish Flying Club during 1928, the Clubs first year of operation. In fact, he was probably the first private owner at Renfrew with his 1920 Boulton and Paul P.9 G-EASJ, the second of its type.

A.C.H. 'Campbell' MacLean had been seconded from his Regiment, the Royal Scots, to the new Royal Flying Corps, Military Wing, in the Autumn of 1912, joining No.4 Squadron at Farnborough. He subsequently transferred to No.2 Squadron at Montrose, thereafter being appointed an instructor, and afterwards Chief Instructor at the embryonic Central Flying School, Upavon. After the outbreak of War, he was with No.1 Squadron and became Commanding Officer of 5 Squadron during October, 1914, in France. His progress was marked by a spell as Commandant, Central Flying School, and in 1918 was appointed Brigadier General and posted to South East Area as its Chief Staff Officer. At this point, his old regiment, much in need of a senior officer, asked him to return, which he did in the Autumn of 1919. Being over age for the Army during the Second World War, he volunteered for the RAF joining as a Pilot Officer and was quickly promoted to Squadron Leader by his AOC, whose wings certificate he had signed as Commandant, CFS, in 1916! Campbell MacLean's nephew, Hector, was one of that élite band who formed the mainstay of 602 (City of Glasgow) Squadron, Auxiliary Air Force, in the mid-1930s, and were to distinguish themselves in 1940 during the Battle of Britain. These, then, were the men who wrote the prologue to the story of Renfrew Airport.

There had been a few hardy souls in Scotland who had attempted flight, by various means, during the preceding centuries, notably, John Damian's celebrated, but unsuccessful leap off the battlements of Stirling Castle in 1507. On the 23rd November, 1785, Vincent Lunardi made an ascent by hot-air balloon from the St. Andrew's Churchyard in Glasgow, to be followed in 1815 by James Sadler, who travelled from Glasgow to Milngavie by similar means. However, it was in 1895 that an assistant lecturer in Naval Architecture at the University of Glasgow, Percy Pilcher, began flying his 'Bat' glider at

excerpts from a chronology of Renfrew, including some other significant events

From Jumpers, Floaters and Flappers to the Jet-age

Moorpark Aerodrome, Renfrew, 1916 -1966, designated Renfrew Airport, early 1933, Scotland's first municipal civil airport.
Abbotsinch, 1933, ex. RAF and RN to Glasgow Airport from 2nd May1966 to present.

1507
John Damian attempted to fly by jumping from Stirling Castle — his wings made from chicken feathers did not support him — he should have used eagle's feathers, as he is reported to have said after surviving the attempt. He would seem to have been Scotland's first 'jumper'.

1783
21 Nov. First aerial voyage — in hot-air, Montgolfier Balloon. F. Pilatre de Rozier and Marquis of Arlandes, at 1.54 p.m. from the Bois de Boulogne, Paris.

1784
25 August. James Tytler made his first ascent in a hot air balloon at Comely Gardens, Edinburgh. Scotland's first 'floater'.

1785
23 November. Vincent Lunardi, having already made several balloon ascents performed in Glasgow from St. Andrew's Churchyard.

1804
From this time Sir George Cayley began flying machines proving his discovery of the lift properties of cambered surfaces — aerodynamics as we now know it.

1815
James Sadler, first English balloonist flew from Glasgow to Milngavie. Not up to Lunardi's achievements.

1866
12 January. Aeronautical Society of Great Britain formed.

1895
Percy Pilcher, assistant lecturer in Naval Architecture at the University of Glasgow, having experimented with models, observed Lillenthal's gliders in Germany and flown in one of them, made the first flight in his own 'Bat' glider at Wallacetown Farm, near Cardross, Dunbartonshire, during early June. Pilcher's method of launching himself off a downward slope must surely make him among the first of the hang glider fraternity.

1896
Pilcher built two more gliders, the 'Beetle' and the 'Gull' in the Spring of that year. Neither were successful however. He left the University about that time and went to Eynsford, Kent, to work with Sir Hiram Maxim, another early aviation pioneer.

There he built a further glider, the 'Hawk', successfully flying it until his tragic death in it on 30th September, 1899. It had been his intention to fit an engine to this glider and had his success continued, who knows, he might well have beaten the Wright Brothers.

1903
17th December, 10.35 a.m. Orville Wright made the world's first sustained and controlled, powered flight from the sand dunes at Kitty Hawk, North Carolina, USA. He was followed the same day by his brother, Wilbur, and together made four successful flights on that auspicious day.

1907
J.W. Dunne brought his experimental swept-wing aircraft to Glen Tilt near Blair Athol for 'secret' trials.

1908
Various experimental attempts at designing and making aeroplanes in Scotland, by the Barnwell Brothers, Preston Watson and the Gibsons. At Barrhead a group established a centre for the development of aviation and rented a field in Aurs Road for experimental flying. The Scottish Aviation Co. was to form here in 1911.

1909
Scottish Aeronautical Society founded. Lasted until 1926, however not related to the Royal Aeronautical Society.
25 July. Louis Bleriot makes first crossing of English Channel by air.
Denny-Mumford helicopter built by Denny's of Dumbarton. Not successful however — would have been the world's first pure helicopter — E.R. Mumford had begun his experiments in 1905.

1910
Prize offered by Mr. J.K. Law for the first flight of half a mile by a Scottish aeroplane — won by Frank Barnwell on 30th January for a flight of over one mile.
Scotland's first flying meeting at Lanark Racecourse from 6th — 13th August, organised by the Scottish Aeronautical Society. Twenty-two pilots and twenty-six aircraft participated and competed, including James Radley, who had already given Glasgow its first public demonstration of powered flight in the grounds of Pollok House, some two months previously.
During the event, J. Armstrong Drexel, flying a Bleriot type monoplane achieved a height of 6,750 ft. The famous 'Colonel' S.F. Cody was there! Over 200,000 people paid to get in during the week.
W. & S. Pollock of Glasgow built a Bleriot type aircraft with a 60 h.p. engine of their own design — it didn't fly!

1911
Flying schools established at Lanark and Barrhead, by the Lanark School of Aviation on 13th May and the Scottish Aviation Company on 3rd June respectively. The latter company had A.V. Roe and C.G. Grey among its Directors and Walter Duncan, Secretary to the Scottish Aviation Society. This year saw the first Round Britain Air Race, sponsored by the 'Daily Mail'. One of the alighting places was the old Paisley Racecourse on the Greenock Road — what became St. James Park. Again, Samuel Cody (not to be confused with 'Buffalo Bill' Cody) was in Glasgow. About 20,000 people turned out to spectate.
Around this time, the Royal Engineers were trying out Balloons in the Leuchars area.
9-26 Sept. First regular service by air between two points in the UK — mail flights celebrating the Coronation of H.M. King George V between Hendon and the Royal Farm at Windsor — profitable — it made £1438!

Wallacetown Farm, Cardross. He continued his experiments with further gliders, leaving the University during 1896 and began working with the inventor and pioneer aviator, Sir Hiram Maxim at Eynsford, Kent. In 1899 he was successfully flying his 'Hawk' glider with, it would seem, the intention of fitting an engine to it, when tragically, he was killed in it on 30th September — he might just have beaten the Wrights who actually did on 17th December, 1903.

With the establishment of a Ministry of Munitions in 1915, a great expansion scheme was inaugurated to produce aircraft and engines for the Royal Flying Corps and Royal Naval Air Service. On Clydeside, not only Beardmore's, who had already become involved in aircraft and engine production, but many others including, inevitably, non-aviation firms, began to build a number of standard types of aircraft.

The lands at Newmains Farm and Porterfield would seem to have been owned by Renfrew Town Council, the farm being tenanted by Mr. John Campbell under leases due to expire at Martinmas, 1917, and Whitsunday, 1918. The first indication of official action regarding their use for official military purposes is noted in the minutes of the Property and Improvement Committee of 6th March, 1916, which notes that an order under the Defence of the Realm Regulations 1914, requires that "no ploughing should take place in certain portions of the lands of Newmains belonging to the Burgh, amounting to 19 acres. The tenant, Mr. Campbell, had been informed". From then on, the minutes of various Council Committees recorded the progress of the 'new Government Works at Newmains' and the word aerodrome is actually mentioned with regard to sanitation at the meeting of the Public Health Committee on 15th June, 1916. During the Great War, official secrecy, endemic in British affairs, then as now, severely limited public knowledge of what was going on, though it must have been fairly obvious, when buildings were being erected. On 13th March, 1916, the Town Council agreed to insure the Town Hall, Police buildings and Gas Works against damage by aircraft.

Towards the end of the year and during January and February, 1917, negotiations continued between the Town Council and the War Office, in the person of Colonel C.B. Dudgeon in Edinburgh, regarding the land at Newmains taken by the Ministry of Munitions, and ended with the agreement that arrangements 'relative to a temporary occupation by Government should be conducted solely with the tenants'. Col. Dudgeon had also stated that, 'occupation of the required land in connection with the aerodrome would cease after the termination of the War', and that compensation for the trees, etc. which had been removed would be reserved, 'till the re-instatement of the tenant in the possession of the whole farm.' Further correspondence in August, 1917, with Col. Dudgeon ensued, regarding the ground at Newmains Farm, 'taken off Mr. Campbell's farm for Aerodrome Sheds', and previous discussions regarding a small camp, 'being established at the Moorpark Aerodrome' suggest increasing activity at the newly named airfield. It is not easy, however, to be precise as to when either military flying commenced or the original hangars were built and brought into use. There was considerable activity at the Newmains site, which came to be called the Moorpark Aerodrome, from the Spring of 1916 until after the Armistice. Indeed at the Council Meeting on 11th November, 1918, Armistice Day, Messrs. Patterson and Sim, agents for Campbell the tenant, were still negotiating on his behalf. Campbell had the farm steading until May, 1919, however, he had left Newmains during that year's New Year week leaving the farm locked-up.

By February 1919, Renfrew's Town Clerk had had a meeting with the Scottish Command Land Agent with a view to letting that part of the farm not taken over by the RAF, as a dairy farm — the land agent had no instructions from the RAF as to them taking over the whole farm. By the 19th of the month, Campbell had left the steading and five and a half acres which was still in the hands of the Burgh. The Town Council decided to let this land on a year-to-year basis as a dairy farm and on 3rd March, 1919, it was let to a Miss Jenny Gilchrist. She and her sister were great characters and the, 'Gilchrist girls' were to be seen all over the district in their Morris Cowley car and were still there in the late 1950s, despite the considerable developments which had taken place at Renfrew.

What to do then with the airfield and its hutted camp? Correspondence ensued between the Air Ministry's Directorate of Lands and Renfrew Town Council during June, 1920, with the former enquiring as to whether the Council were interested in granting a lease of the airfield for civil aviation purposes. On 2nd August, 1920, the Council's Property and Improvement Committee recommended that Renfrew Town Council offer the Air Ministry a lease of the Aerodrome at Moorpark for five years, for civil flying at an annual rental of £3.10s.0d. per acre, subject to tenants giving up on a three months' notice. A report in the Glasgow Herald of 16th September, 1921, from a meeting of the Scottish Branch of the Royal Aeronautical Society makes intriguing reading. During the previous year, the Society had been expressing its concern for the futures of the 'Renfrew and Inchinnan' aerodromes . Several interviews had taken place with the Ministry of Munitions Disposal Board with, ultimately the Air Ministry, announcing that the Renfrew Reception Park (i.e. aerodrome) would be retained on a five years' lease. At Inchinnan, only the ground on which Messrs. Beardmore's works stood would be retained. The Ministry had requested the co-operation of the Society with regard to securing Renfrew's future, 'as a permanent home of aviation in the West of Scotland' — using its good offices to co-ordinate the interests of various local authorities. 'It was intended that the movement in regard to securing the necessary co-ordination of all parties interested, would be proceeded in the near future'. This report sheds an interesting light upon the negotiations between the Air Ministry and Renfrew Town Council. Eventually in August, 1923, agreement was reached and the Air Ministry was granted a five year lease of the aerodrome from Whitsunday, 1923, at a rental of £5 per acre — the increased rent being due to the Council agreeing to drop certain of the previous terms. The camp had been demolished by August, 1921.

Thus the Moorpark aerodrome and its hangars, RFC General Service Aeroplane Sheds came into being. These hangars remained until the end of flying at

1912
Various enthusiasts continued flying in Scotland using French machines, during the period up to the outbreak of the First World War.
13 April. Royal Flying Corps. founded by Royal Warrant. It was composed of Military and Naval Wings. Airfield established at Montrose by R.F.C., the first military airfield in Scotland.

1913
No.2 Squadron RFC based at Montrose. 5 aircraft flying from Farnborough to Montrose.
Licence to construct Austro-Daimler aero engines obtained by William Beardmore & Co. — over 2,800 of them were to be produced.
Around this time James G. Weir was experimenting with aircraft on farmland in the Renfrew/Moorpark area and it is suggested that a Lt. A.C.H. MacLean of the RFC, a Glasgow man and 'landings officer' of his Squadron selected that area for an airfield — the beginning of Renfrew Airport.
Beardmore's expressed their interest in aviation by obtaining a licence to construct the German DFW aeroplane, buying two of them.

1914
January. Air Ministry established in which a Civil Aviation Department would be formed.
June 25th - 28th. Scottish Aeronautical Society's flying meeting at Scotstoun during which a new Scottish height record of 7,100 feet was claimed. It was also very profitable for the Society.
Beardmore's take out licence to produce the German DFW biplane — not taken up due to subsequent international events.
1 July. Naval Wing of RFC becomes Royal Naval Air Service.
4 Aug. Outbreak of First World War which, inevitably, was a great spur to aeronautical development.
Expansion scheme for aeroplane production using subcontractors not necessarily involved in aviation introduced.
G. & J. Weir of Glasgow, first Clydeside and non-aero firm to receive contracts, for BE2c, FE2b, and DH9 aeroplanes. Also involved were the Clyde shipyards, Barclay-Curle, Dennys and Fairfields.

1915
Wm. Beardmore Ltd. had received large contracts for aeroplane construction — production begins at Dalmuir early in the year.
During the middle of 1915, Scottish built aircraft were beginning to be seen test flying. Beardmore's used field at Dalmuir and later at Inchinnan for test flying purposes, the latter becoming famous for its airship construction. The real beginning of a Scottish Aircraft industry. First Beardmore built aircraft, a BE2C delivered 8th March,   No.1099.
26 May. Asquith's new Coalition Government in being, Lloyd George becomes Minister of Munitions, a new office — Munitions of War Act, July 1915.
14 July. William Weir (G. & J. Weir, Cathcart, Glasgow) appointed Director of Munitions, Scotland. Later Director of Aeronautical Supplies and Secretary of State for Air — 1st Viscount Weir of Eastwood — 1938.

1916

During 1916 it would seem that the Ministry of Munitions (of War) began the establishment of an aerodrome on the lands of Newmains Farm, Renfrew. G. & J. Weir transferred their tests from a field at Carmunnock to Renfrew, probably in the summer or autumn. Beardmore, however, constructed two small hangars during this year, at Robertson's Park, adjacent to their Dalmuir works for the final assembly and flying off of aircraft, to Inchinnan.

6 March. From the Minutes of Renfrew Town Council, a Mr. John Campbell, tenant of Newmains Farm was ordered under Defence of the Realm Regulations 1914, to cease ploughing on certain parts of the Lands of Newmains belonging to the Council.

1 May. Plans for work at Newmains submitted.

5 June. Contractors at Newmains preparing to erect further buildings.

Beardmore's inaugurate their own design department with the appointment of George Tilghman Richards, previously with the Admiralty as H.M. Director of Naval Aircraft. His first aircraft was the W.B.I biplane bomber of which only one was built. It was followed by the W.B.II, a development of the B.E.2s produced in large numbers. A conversion to the Sopwith Pup became the W.B.III. Beardmores had become a significant force in the aeroplane , airship and engine design, and production.

Meanwhile at Inchinnan, a large airship shed was built, in connection with the airship design and construction undertaken by Beardmores. The erection of the first airship No.24 beginning on 21st July. An aircraft acceptance park was also established at Inchinnan.

11 Dec. Reference in Town Council Minutes to correspondence from Col. Dudgeon as to ground used for 'aerodrome sheds' at Newmains.

1917

19 April. Plans for 'small camp' to be erected at 'Moorpark Aerodrome'.

28 Oct. Airship No. 24 commissioned into Royal Naval Air Service. On this day, eight soldiers posted in to Renfrew from No. 2 Aircraft Depot.

2 Nov. '6th Aircraft Park R.F.C.' in being at Renfrew, 6 officers and 135 other ranks under Major A.F. A. Hooper (this officer had received the O.B.E. by Feb. 1919).

1918

10 March. Establishment of No. 6 (Glasgow) Aircraft Acceptance Park and No. 6 (Scottish) Aircraft and Engine Repair Depot at Renfrew. (See also 2 Nov. 1917).

1 April. Royal Air Force brought into being from the amalgamation of the R.F.C. and R.N.A.S.

13 May. References in Town Council Minutes to new 'Government Aerodrome Works' at Moorpark.

9 Sept. Letter (to Renfrew Town Council) from the C.O. 'Renfrew Aerodrome' asking for a note of charges for attendance of Fire Brigade.

17 Oct. First Sopwith 2F-1 Camel, N7140, aircraft built by Arrol-Johnston at Heathall, Dumfries (sub-contract from Beardmores) delivered to 6.A.A.P. at Renfrew.

At last, at 11 a.m. on 11th November, the Great War came to an end. The future for peaceful, civil aviation looked bright. It was not to be, at least initially. Though many enterprises were begun, few succeeded in the immediate aftermath of the War. The need for aircraft also had vanished.

Renfrew and for a few years thereafter. What an opportunity there was then, to create a small local history museum! The original grass airfield was bounded on the north by Newmains Road and to the south by Arkleston Cemetery and farm.

During the First World War, the establishment of an 'acceptance field' in the West of Scotland was made necessary by the expansion of aircraft and aero-engine production on Clydeside. Beardmore's, one of the main UK armament firms had begun their aeronautical activities before the First World War, obtained a licence to build the German DFW aeroplane, and at Dalmuir, their aviation division built various of the early aircraft such as the B.E.2c under sub-contract. Significantly, they also created their own design organisation, eventually producing modifications to existing aircraft such as a Beardmore modified Sopwith Pup for naval use and a shipboard version of the Sopwith Camel, together with a number of their own designs. Initial flying took place at Robertson's Park, Dalmuir, adjacent to their works where two hangars were built during 1916. Beardmore also established airship construction at Inchinnan during 1916, producing, among others, the Atlantic record breaking R34. They also assembled and test flew there, the Dalmuir built Handley Page V/1500 Bombers. At what is titled 'RN Inchinnan' on the plans, another Aircraft Acceptance Park was established and a hangar built alongside the airship construction shed. Both Dalmuir and Inchinnan were closed in 1921. The first Beardmore built aircraft, a B.E.2c, probably No. 1099, was delivered on 8th March, 1915.

Meanwhile, G. & J. Weir at Cathcart was the first 'non-aero' company to receive orders for aircraft, initially for B.E.2cs which were taken up the hill to a field at Carmunnock for test flying. Weirs went on to build F.E.2bs and D.H.9s, and a total of 1427 aircraft during the war period, (including those involved in the group production scheme actually built outwith Weirs). It was probably during 1916 that Weirs transferred their test flying to Renfrew.

On the Clyde, Barclay Curle's at Whiteinch built a total of 325 B.E.2cs, F.E.2bs, Sopwith Snipes and Fairey Campanias; Dennys at Dumbarton, 150 B.E.2cs; Fairfields at Govan, 100 Sopwith Cuckoos; and Stephens at Linthouse, 150 F.E.2bs. It is likely that most of these aircraft would be 'accepted' at the Moorpark aerodrome, Renfrew.

By 2nd November, 1917, No.6 Aircraft Acceptance Park, Royal Flying Corps, was in being at Moorpark. Its complement comprised 6 officers and 135 other ranks, and in its field return for that day, under an intriguing sub-heading of 'natives', noted 1 RAMC and 5 RFC personnel. It would appear that the Commanding Officer was Major A.F.A. Hooper and that 'the 6th Aircraft Park comes under the Command of the Officer Commanding 41st Wing with effect from 28.10.17'. Field returns were made to the Officer i/c RFC Section, GHQ 3rd Echelon. When the associated No.6 Aircraft and Engine Repair Depot closed on 19th February, 1919, Major Hooper was still there, having been awarded the OBE. The Aircraft Acceptance Park, was not officially closed until March, 1920.

Beardmore built Handley Page V/1500 bomber with Beardmore's developed version of the Sopwith Camel, at Inchinnan.

Beardmore built B.E.2c at Dalmuir 1917(?).

Beardmore W.B. V, single seat fighter at Dalmuir, late 1917/early 1918.

Airship R34 at Inchinnan where she was built by Beardmores. She completed the first return crossing of the Atlantic in July 1919.

Beardmore W.B.IIB, two seater. This aircraft was used on the proving flight of Beardmore's experimental Renfrew to Croydon service on 17th September 1920.

Beardmore W.B. XXIV 'The Wee Bee' at Renfrew. This aircraft won the Air Ministry's light aeroplane competition at Lympne in October 1924.

Blackburn Kangaroos at Renfrew, 8th September 1922(?), G-EAIU and G-EAMJ. Despite reports that neither of these aircraft reached Renfrew during the King's Cup Air Race on 8th September 1922 this photograph shows them both there.

1919

6 Jan. Mr Campbell vacated Newmains Farm.

19 Feb. Closure of No.6 Aircraft and Engine Repair Depot.

3 March. Miss Gilchrist takes the let of Newmains Farm on a year-to-year basis (she was still there with her sisters in the 1950s!).

30th April. Air Navigation Regulations promulgated and aerodromes selected for civil use. Routes proposed including main trunk routes to Glasgow (Renfrew) and Edinburgh (Turnhouse) and including one between them.

1 May. Civil flying now permitted though some who had been done during the Easter.

First UK domestic service flight by Handley Page Ltd. H.P. 0/400 D8350 still with its military serial number from London (Cricklewood) to Didsbury, Carlisle, Dundee, Montrose and Aberdeen, then Edinburgh for a night stop — newspapers were dropped en route. Sholto Douglas, the pilot, as Lord Douglas of Kirtleside, was to become Chairman of B.E.A. after World War II. Due to weather, the northbound sectors from Manchester didn't take place until 5th May.

12 May. A number of flights had already been made by Handley Page Ltd. 0/400 aircraft between Glasgow (Renfrew) and Manchester delivering newspapers. On this day F-5414, flown by Capt. W. Shakespeare on this route, crashed on take-off at Harker after a forced landing — no injuries.

15 June. Alcock and Brown make first non-stop crossing of the Atlantic by air in Vickers Vimy, the 1900 miles from Newfoundland to Ireland taking 16 hours and 12 minutes.

July. Airship R34 built by Beardmore's at Inchinnan, completed first double crossing of the Atlantic from East Fortune (2nd July), back to Pulham (due to bad weather at East Fortune, 13th July).

25 Aug. World's first scheduled international air service inaugurated by George Holt Thomas' Aircraft Transport and Travel — Hounslow Heath to Paris in single engined DH16 converted bomber, K.130 (later G-EACT) piloted by Major Patterson.

24 Sept. Scottish Branch of Royal Aeronautical Society formed.

29 Sept.-6 Oct. Railway strike. During the strike, Aircraft Transport & Travel D.H.10 G-EAJO operated London — Renfrew mail service.

13th Nov. Paris Air Convention produced 'Regulations relating to Air Navigation'. These became law in UK by virtue of Air Navigation Act, supervised by Civil Aviation Dept. of Air Ministry.

Air Commodore James Weir's Cierva Autogiro at Renfrew around 1928. Weir became considerably involved with Cierva in Autogyro development particularly up to the outbreak of World War 2. James G. Weir was in fact instrumental in setting up the Cierva Autogyro Co. becoming its first chairman, a post he still held into the 1960s.

Armstrong Whitworth Argosy I, G-EBLF 'City of Glasgow'. This aircraft made a number of visits to Renfrew in the late 1920s and early thirties and on each occasion was flown by the legendary Capt. O.P. Jones of Imperial Airways. On one day, he carried more than 1000 passengers over Glasgow in this machine.

T H E

T E N T A T I V E

T W E N T I E S

MOORPARK aerodrome played an active part in supporting the new aviation activities on Clydeside for a period of about three years. By 1920, however, it was empty and had been abandoned, with only the vivacious Gilchrist girls to enliven the scene. It took until 1923 for the Air Ministry to finally conclude its leasing arrangements with the very astute Renfrew Town Council. Civil flying, was taking just as long to begin establishing itself, even with the impetus which the war had provided.

Beardmore's, it is true, had made a number of proving flights with their own W.B.IIB aircraft between Glasgow (Moorpark) and London (Croydon). One was recorded on 17th September 1920, by G-EARY, and another on 5th November by its sister, G-EARX to London (Cricklewood). By 1921, in difficult times, Beadmore's — temporarily — closed their aviation division.

A brighter note was struck on 8th September, 1922, when the first King's Cup air race included a stop at the Moorpark aerodrome. First to land was Capt. F.L. Barnard in the D.H.4a G-EAMU and he was presented to the Lord Provost of the City of Glasgow, Lord Weir, Sir Thomas Lipton and the Chief of the Air Staff, Sir Hugh Trenchard. Barnard went on to win the Cup. Two Blackburn Kangaroo aircraft participated in the race — G-EAMJ entered by the Rt. Hon. Winston Churchill, MP, and flown by Lt.-Col. Spencer Grey and G-EAIU flown by R.W. Kenworthy. Although they were reported to have got no further than Newcastle when lack of light stopped play, a photograph, which surely must have been taken at the time of the race, shows them at Renfrew, and contradicts this report.

It was Beardmore's who brought the airfield back to life by establishing an RAF Reserve Flying School there on 23rd July, 1923. That great Clydeside firm also restarted its own aviation division, employing W.S. Shackleton as designer. He became well known in the trade later and won the Air Ministry's Light Aeroplane Competition at Lympne in the October of 1924, with his W.B.XXIV Wee Bee. It was superceded by de Havilland's Moth, a type which would see much service at Renfrew.

In 1923, William Beardmore & Co. Ltd. was appointed as the firm to manage the Royal Air Force Reserve Flying School in the Scottish district, at Renfrew Aerodrome.

The officers called up for training came under two categories: those in flying practice, who were required to put in a minimum of twelve hours solo flying per year on Service aircraft, and those former officers of the RAF who had not flown for some time, and required a re-qualifying course of flying training. Re-qualifying course pupils were required to undergo, 'very extensive and

Beardmore's RAF Reserve Flying School, Renfrew.
Group in front of Bristol Type 89, G-EBNZ, c. 1926.
2nd from left - A.N. Kingwill
3rd from left - Ramsay
4th from left - John Houston (Asst. Inst.)
2nd from right -M. O'Flaherty (Chief Engineer)
3rd from right - Walker.

'Mr. Loudon, Beardmore's Flying School'.
Mr. J.M. Loudon, Beardmore's manager of its Aviation Division at Renfrew with one of Beardmore's 'Renfrew Flying School's' Bristol Type 89As, G-EBSB.

Avro 504K of Beardmore's at Renfrew. c. 1923-4.

Flying Officer A.N. Kingwill (on ladder) instructs his class at Beardmore's RAF Flying School, Renfrew, 1923.

D.H.9C of Beardmore's Flying School at Renfrew around 1923/24.

Bristol Type 89A, G-EBOD, of Beardmore's Renfrew, crashed on railway embankment, Pollokshaws, Glasgow, on 26th May, 1927.

minute' training on Avro 504Ks, followed by five hours solo on de Havilland D.H.9s, including one cross-country flight of sixty miles. Ground training consisted of lectures on meteorology, wireless, rigging, engine overhaul and general workshop practice.

The Renfrew school was opened on 23rd July, 1923, and Mr. A.J. Campbell, the general manager of Beardmore's Dalmuir works, was placed in charge. The pilot instructors were Flight Lieutenant A.N. Kingwill (who was Beardmore's chief pilot) and Captain J.C. Houston, MC, and the manager was Mr. R.C. Russell, late of the company's Aircraft Works at Dalmuir and Inchinnan. Russell was later succeeded by Mr. J.M. Loudon.

The hangars at Renfrew were fully equipped with engine test benches and electric power. Beardmore supplied a competent staff of mechanics and riggers, who held the requisite ground engineers' licences. In its original form the school could train eighty pupils per annum, but there was capacity for expansion.

In December, 1923, *The Aeroplane* reported that the school had three Avro 504Ks powered by 110 h.p. Le Rhône rotary engines, and three D.H.9s powered by 240 h.p. Siddeley Pumas, all six aircraft being fitted with dual controls. A complete stock of aircraft and engine spares was held in the aerodrome workshops, and a thousand-gallon bulk storage petrol system was specially installed.

Although the weather from July to September, 1923, was the worst on record for the West, and there were only three dry days during October, the school was constantly busy, and by early December, 27 pupils had passed the prescribed course.

From June, 1926, the school began to re-equip with Bristol Type 89 and Type 89A trainers, powered by 320 h.p. Bristol Jupiter radial engines. These biplanes were descendants of the famous Bristol Fighter of the First World War and were often known, misleadingly, as Bristol Fighters by those who flew them. Although the school had seven Bristol 89s, it never relinquished all of its 504Ks and D.H.9s, and four of the former and one of the latter, served alongside their 'replacements'.

One trainee made comparative notes on the flying qualities of the 504K and the 'Bristol Fighter'. The Avro's balanced rudder was delicate and quick in response, needing 'gentle operation', while that of the Type 89 was heavy and required firm operation. Conversely, the Avro's ailerons were heavy and slow to respond, and needed rudder to counteract their drag, while the Bristol's ailerons were 'very efficient' and responded quickly because there were balanced, though they caused 'a great yawing motion'. The elevators of the two types were similar in action. As a result of these differences, the Avro required careful use of the rudder in turns, while the Type 89's rudder needed firm use 'to counteract the great aileron drag'. The gyroscopic action of the Avro's rotary engine demanded more rudder in a turn to the right that in a turn to the left. There was practically no gyroscopic effect in the Type 89.

An adjustable tailplane enabled the Bristol pilot to get the best conditions for climbing, level flight, or gliding, and its engine controls were much better than those of the Avro's Le Rhône rotary, which could not be throttled down, only 'blipped' on and off.

A total of seventeen different aircraft, all civil registered, were used through the Renfrew School's lifetime — six Avro 504Ks, three D.H.9s, one D.H.9c, two Bristol Type 89s, G-EBOA and G-EBOD, which had been crashed, plus spares. There were never more than eight or nine aircraft in use at any one time.

Beardmore's RAF Reserve Flying School was closed down in November, 1928, though a few aircraft flew on into 1929.

It is fitting to conclude with a brief recollection by A.N. Kingwill:

> I was Chief Flying Instructor of the School throughout its life. Several of these schools were formed throughout the country in 1923, when the Reserve of Air Force Officers was instituted. Since all Reservists had previous flying experience, there was very little *ab initio* training in the early years, but we agreed to teach a number of aspirants to the local Auxiliary Air Force Squadron who, having been accepted as suitable candidates for commissions, were required to obtain Private Pilot's Licences before being finally enlisted. The cost of tuition was refunded to them if they got their licences, but not if they failed! I do not remember any failures, as they were most excellent pilot material, as was later proved by their wonderful war records.
>
> When the school was finally closed in 1928, I received yet another commemorative cigarette case from my Scottish friends of the R.A.F.O.

In 1929, Kingwill was in charge of flying operations for Northern Air Lines at Manchester, and he became the Manager of Manchester Municipal Airport. John Houston, one of the other instructors, became Chief Flying Instructor of the Renfrew-based Scottish Flying Club. Kingwill returned to Renfrew to perform stunt flying in one of his company's — Kingwill and Jones' Mongoose Avro 504s.

The 12th of September, 1925, was a rather miserable day for weather at Renfrew. That day, however, saw the actual inauguration of the Auxiliary Air Force. The first squadron of that illustrious force, which would play such a crucial role in its country's survival, was about to be formed. For it was on that Saturday morning at Renfrew, that Flight Lieutenant Gilbert 'Dan' Martyn took up his post as regular adjutant of number 602, (City of Glasgow) Squadron, Auxiliary Air Force. It was part of Trenchard's vision for the RAF to create an equivalent to the Territorial Army and make a 'Corps d'Elite'. In that, as events would prove, he succeeded admirably.

The Air Ministry's lease of the Moorpark aerodrome was thus most convenient in allowing the City of Glasgow Squadron to form quickly and its first aircraft, a D.H.9a light bomber was delivered from Henlow on 7th October by 602's first Commanding Officer, C.N. Lowe — a regular officer and a noted RAF rugby, wing three-quarter. 602's first Auxiliary Commanding Officer, J.D.Latta, was not available until the following February. The Squadron attracted not only an 'elite' of officers but also of NCOs and airmen. George Pinkerton, who was to join in 1933 was emphatic about the high quality of engineering skill possessed by 602 — a natural characteristic of the West of Scotland. He gave up speedway racing for the rather 'safer' sport of flying and, as a Flight Commander in 602, was responsible for shooting-down the first enemy aircraft over the United Kingdom on l6th October, 1939, shortly after the outbreak of the Second World War. His wingman on the day was the indefatigable, Archie McKellar — sadly, he was to lose his life just a few hours after the Battle of Britain was 'officially' declared finished. Many of these 'weekend flyers' who joined 602 Squadron in its early days at Renfrew and, after January 1933 at Abbotsinch, went on to create for the City of Glasgow Squadron, an honourable place in the annals and history of the Royal Auxiliary Air Force and military flying. The Marquess of Douglas and Clydesdale, (later l4th Duke of Hamilton), joining in 1927, became Commanding Officer in 1932, to be followed by David McIntyre in 1936. They were the first men to fly over Mount Everest in 1933, and went on to found Scottish Aviation Ltd. at Prestwick and develop the international airport there. 'Sandy' Johnstone, School Captain at Kelvinside Academy, commanded the Squadron during the tense days of the Battle of Britain, when 602 went south to Tangmere's satellite Westhampnett, and with him were those other pre-war stalwarts, Dunlop Urie, Hector MacLean, Donald Jack and Paul Webb. George Pinkerton had become, by then, the first auxiliary officer to command a regular RAF Squadron, No.65 (he would return to command 602). Marcus Robinson had been posted to command 616, the South Yorkshire Auxiliary Squadron, though his association with 602 would be long indeed, as he re-formed it in 1946 after the War. Douglas Farquhar, 602's CO at the outbreak of war and Archie McKellar had also been promoted elsewhere to fight.

Renfrew, in the late 1920s was too small even for the D.H.9as, Fairey Fawns and Westland Wapitis with which 602 was successively equipped. A new airfield was required and a site at Abbotsinch was chosen. They moved there from Renfrew in January, 1933. Abbotsinch was to see great changes in the Squadron's equipment — from the Wapiti to the beautiful Hawker Hart and then Hind light bombers and, in a brief change of role, the Army Co-operation Hector. It was in January, 1939, that 602 Squadron became a fighter squadron, a role in which it was to create an imperishable record. Equipped at first with the Gloster Gauntlet biplane, on the 8th of May, 1939, at Abbotsinch, the Glasgow Squadron became the first Auxiliary Squadron to be equipped with the RAF's new super fighter, the Supermarine Spitfire and this, ahead of many of the RAF's regular squadrons. The air around the West of Scotland was soon to resound to the song of the Rolls-Royce Merlin engine. 24th August, 1939, saw the Squadron mobilised at Abbotsinch and in October, move temporarily to Grangemouth and then to Drem on the east coast, to protect the naval base at Rosyth and coastal shipping. 602's war record is an

1 →

602 (City of Glasgow) Squadron Auxiliary Air Force at Renfrew, March 1926 shortly after formation.

2 →

602 Squadron Avro 504N, Renfrew 1931 or 1932.

3 →

One of 602's Wapitis in their hangar at Renfrew, 1931.

1

2

3

inspiring one, well recorded elsewhere. Both Renfrew and Abbotsinch played major supporting roles in the war effort. Their location, being convenient to both the Glasgow Docks and the Clyde estuary, making them ideal as aircraft receiving, overhaul and maintenance bases. Thousands of aircraft being shipped to the Clyde in crates, assembled thereafter at Renfrew and flown away.

Renfrew itself was greatly expanded during 1942/43 and proper runways were laid down by the Ministry of Aircraft Production. The Lockheed Company established a base to look after aircraft shipped from the USA to the Clyde. Airwork Ltd. established a major aircraft overhaul facility there. Whilst many of the original air services were continued, under war conditions, the companies were organised initially under the National Air Communcations Scheme and then, within the Associated Airways Joint Committee (AAJC). Walter Bell recounts, later on in this story, the memories of a wartime spotter.

Significantly, Edmund E. Fresson, a former RFC pilot, having returned from China, where he had designed and built an aircraft, went into business with L.J. Rimmer at Hooton Park, Cheshire, in 1928. Their firm, North British Aviation Co. flew Avro 504Ks barnstorming throughout the UK. He visited Dumfries, Renfrew and Ayr, on the 19th, 20th and 23rd July, 1928, returning to Scotland in each of the following four years before setting up Highland Airways at Inverness in 1933, and beginning his pioneering air services on 8th May, 1933. from Inverness (Longman) to Kirkwall, with the Monospar S.T.4 G-ACEW *Inverness*.

Meanwhile, back at Renfrew, in April, 1927, whilst 602 Squadron was becoming established, a group of ex-RFC and RNAS pilots had met in Miss Cranston's tearooms to discuss the formation of a light aeroplane club, a previous attempt by others having failed — the Glasgow Light Aeroplane Club of 1924. The outcome was, the Scottish Flying Club, an organisation which was to become pre-eminent in the light aviation world of the 1930s and to take over the running, management and lease of Renfrew aerodrome at the end of the Air Ministry's lease, after the move of 602 Squadron to Abbotsinch. It is interesting to note that just as a number of enterprising bus operators were moving into commercial aviation, prominent members of the motor trade around Glasgow and Paisley would become leading lights in the Scottish Flying Club — Carlaws, Archie Fraser and Colonel McWilliam of Gillespies, being among them. Col. McWilliam continued his leading role in the Club after the War. The 'Scottish Flyer', the SFC's monthly magazine, is a wonderful record of the times, being published between 1929 and November, 1938. Even more significant is the fact that so many of the 'greats' of 602 Squadron received their necessary initial training with the Club, including George Pinkerton and Archie McKellar. Indeed on the Club's Flying Committee, at the beginning was 602's Adjutant, Flt. Lt. 'Dan' Martyn, together with Messrs. Kingwill, Houston and Jones of the Beardmore Reserve Flying School. Capt. John Houston was to become a much loved and highly respected CFI of the Club. Let Reginald F. Millen, its secretary at that time, tell its story.

T H E   S C O T T I S H
F L Y I N G   C L U B

TAKEN from R.F. Millen's account of 1948 and brought up-to-date by the author.

HOW THE CLUB CAME INTO BEING

THE idea of forming a Flying Club in Scotland, was originally suggested by five men, all ex-pilots, who served in one of the flying Services during the 1914-1918 war, and who were in the habit of meeting for morning coffee in Glasgow. Quite naturally, the chief topic of conversation, was aviation, and the happy times which had been spent in the RFC, RNAS and RAF. At about this time, the Flying Club movement was taking shape, south of the border, and five clubs were already operating. Why not have a Flying Club in Scotland, suggested our friends one day? A good idea, let's get busy. So a Propaganda Committee was formed in April, 1927, comprising the aforesaid five men. They were: Mr. B.R. Millar (RNAS); Mr. G.C. Walker (RFC); Mr. A. Dunlop (RAF) now deceased; Mr. H. Smith (RAF); and Mr. Donaldson (RAF). They were later joined by Mr. G.F. Luke of the Royal Aeronautical Society, Mr. K. Macintosh and Mr. J. Baldwin, who later became the Club's first Secretary.

This Committee was successful in arousing considerable interest among the people in Glasgow and district, to form a Flying Club, so it was decided to appeal for funds. The existing clubs were approached in order to obtain information as to the amount of money required to make a start, and what difficulties were likely to be encountered. It was agreed that the sum of £2,000 would be necessary to ensure a good foundation being laid. This sum was soon forthcoming, thanks to the generosity of many prominent business men, such as Lord Weir (President of the Club), Sir Harold Yarrow, Sir Maurice Denny, and Mr. James Weir, to name just a few.

On 3rd November, 1927, the Scottish Flying Club was born and housed at Renfrew Airport, Renfrew, in the single-bay hangar, which formed its Clubrooms and offices. The first aircraft purchased, was the Cirrus Moth G-EBUU which was flown from Stag Lane, London to Renfrew by a Club Member. In addition, Mr. J.G. Weir, kindly lent the Club his own Cirrus Moth G-EBIQ. In order to stimulate further interest, the first machine was exhibited in Glasgow by Messrs. Wylie & Lochhead, which brought many applications for membership. The first Flying Instructor was one Bob Stirling, who had been employed by Beardmores at the Airport. He was succeeded by 'Red Hot' Jones. Under the guidance of Mr. J.G. Weir as Chairman, and Mr. J. Baldwin as Secretary, the Club became firmly established and made considerable progress during the first year of its life. All members worked

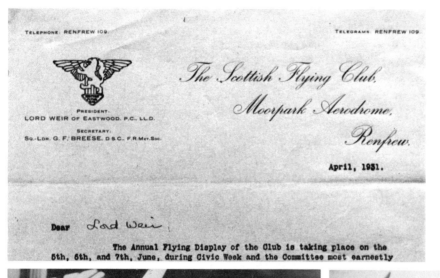

John Houston Chief Flying Instructor of the Scottish Flying Club and gentleman.

Winnie Drinkwater pilot and engineer at Renfrew — Scottish Flying Club.

One of the Scottish Flying Club's Moths at Renfrew 1931/2.

1 →
The Scottish Flying Club's workshops at Renfrew, D.H. Moth being overhauled.
2 →
Brian Millar, Winnie Drinkwater and George Walker of the Scottish Flying Club, Winnie having just won the Mobiloil Cup, 4th October 1931.

1

2

Cierva C.19 Mk. IVP Autogiro, being flown by R.(Reggie) A.C. Brie at one of the Scottish Flying Club's Air Pageants.

Fairey Flycatcher, Air Pageant, 1931.

Handley Page W.8b, G-EBBI, of Imperial Airways at Renfrew during the Scottish Flying Club's Air Pageant, 5-7th June, 1931.

Imperial Airways Westland Wessex at Renfrew, 1932.

M&SAF pilot Noel Mavrogordato's Bristol Fighter at Renfrew in 1931.

Barnard's Air Circus, 1931.

Renfrew aerodrome, early 1930s.

Renfrew, early 1930s.

33

hard, and a great deal of the success was due to the House Committee, the Convenor of which was Mrs. J.F. Mackenzie, assisted by Mrs. C. Millar. Although the Clubrooms consisted only of a portion of the hangar, partitioned off, a great deal of fun was had.

On 23rd February, 1928, the Scottish Flying Club was formed into a Company Limited by Guarantee, the original five members of the Propaganda Committee being subscribers to the Articles of Association.

By the end of 1930, the Club was in a very sound financial position, thanks to the generous nature of its members, who had been invited to subscribe to an Establishment Fund, which at this time stood at over £9,000. New machines were purchased and money invested.

In May, 1933, the Club was granted a 5 years lease for the entire aerodrome and buildings at Renfrew by the Renfrew Town Council, and it was agreed that the Club should act as Managers for the Council. Aviation in Scotland was gaining ground at this time, and several operating Companies were based at Renfrew, including Midland & Scottish Air Ferries Ltd., Hillman's Airways Ltd., and Northern and Scottish Airways Ltd. The last named of company was started by Mr. George Nicholson, and later became known as Scottish Airways Ltd., North Eastern Airways Ltd., came to Renfrew during 1938. In addition to managing the aerodrome, the Scottish Flying Club was responsible to the Air Ministry for Air Traffic Control. The Club trained Control Officers, who undertook their duties to the complete satisfaction of all concerned. The Secretary of the Club filled the three roles of Secretary, Aerodrome Manager and Chief Control Officer. It says a great deal for the efficiency of the Control Staff, of whom there were only three, including the Chief Control Officer, when it is considered that some thirty passenger machines were handled every day in the summer months (Sundays excepted) in addition to Club flying, without mishap. Weather observations were reported from Renfrew every hour. It was not until April, 1939, that the Air Ministry installed its own Air Traffic Control Station, with six officers.

The writer well remembers the many calls for the Air Ambulance machine during the night and early morning, when he lived on the aerodrome. Capt. David Barclay, the Chief Pilot would come knocking at the door at some early hour, with the news that there was a charter to Islay or Campbeltown, and flares were required, also a weather report. As Airport Manager, the writer would assist with the flares, and as Chief Control Officer, get weather reports, and stand by all the time the machine was out, give fixes and any other information required, and finally help get the flares in (they were the old fashioned kind with buckets filled with oil and cotton waste). Back to bed again for an hour or two, then up again for the early morning newspaper runs to the Isle of Man, to be followed with obtaining route forecasts for the scheduled services. It was hard going, but enjoyable. The job was done without fuss or bother, and all concerned played their part, and what is more, all services were out on time and no delay, unless the weather was very bad. The public knew that they could rely upon getting to their destination at the time stated.

Handley Page H.P.42 airliner at Renfrew for the SFC's 1933 Pageant, 602 Squadron fly overhead in their Wapitis.

Westland Wapitis of 602 Squadron taking-off from Renfrew around 1932. Arkleston Cemetry in background.

It was obvious that the Club required larger and better accommodation, as the membership had increased rapidly, so plans were drawn up to erect premises on the side of the four-bay hangar. This new building cost over £6,000 with new furnishings and comprised Dining Room, Kitchen, Stores, Lounge, Smokeroom and Bar, Offices, First Aid Room — fully equipped, toilets and cloakrooms, and a shop where flying equipment was obtainable. New crockery and cutlery was purchased and engraved with the Club's badge. A special floor was laid in the Lounge for dances, dictaphones installed, also loud speakers from a radiogram to the Bar and Dining Room. The whole building was centrally heated. Besides the main building, there was a separate building where members could reside. This new club accommodation was opened in 1934, and was considered to be one of the finest Flying Club

De Havilland D.H.60GIII Moth of the Scottish Flying Club, Renfrew 1933/4.

Fullerton Trophy — Sunday, 5th May, 1935.
Air race between 602 Squadron and Scottish Flying Club — 602 not allowed 'officially' to enter. However, they were well represented by their Scottish Flying Club members!

The Scottish Flying Club visit Islay, July, 1934.

Sunday at the Scottish Flying Club in the mid 1930s.
De Havilland Moths and the tail of a Hornet Moth.

First aerial delivery of pork sausages (McKean's, the Glasgow butcher's, of course) to Arbroath/Montrose by G-ABGM, Alan McKean's D.H. Gipsy Moth.
2nd from left - George Pinkerton
3rd from left - Alan McKean.

Magister, Scottish Flying Club, Renfrew. c. 1952/53/54.

Miles Messenger, G-AJDF, and Magister, (Hawk Trainer III), G-AJRV, of the Scottish Flying Club at Renfrew, c. 1955.

Magister of the Scottish Flying Club at Renfrew, 1955.

premises in the country. Anyone visiting Renfrew was sure of a good welcome, excellent meals and generous hospitality.

The Club's fleet of aircraft was gradually increased and comprised eleven machines, including three aircraft with enclosed cabins, by the time war started in 1939.

The Club did everything possible to encourage flying in Scotland, and for several consecutive years, organised flying displays, which lasted for three days. These were a great attraction, and drew huge crowds. Not only did the Club augment its funds, but the local hospitals also benefited, as part of the proceeds were donated to them. Many members were enrolled, after enjoying their first trip in the air at these meetings.

MEMBERSHIP

There were two classes of membership, Pilot and Associate and by September, 1939, the Club had 210 Pilot Members and 320 Associate Members. Although flying was the chief concern of the Club, the social side was not neglected. Dances were held in the Lounge, also Bridge Parties and Whist Drives. Treasure Hunts were organised, and Badminton was a popular pastime of an evening.

The Scottish Flying Club trained many now famous pilots, one of the best known in Scotland, being Capt. David Barclay, MBE. He created something of a record, by going solo after only 4 hours dual. He later served in the RAF in India, and was afterwards Chief Pilot with Scottish Airways Ltd., until British European Airways took over. The Marquis of Clydesdale and Hamilton (later the Duke of Hamilton) was a Club pupil, and at one time commanded No. 602 City of Glasgow Auxiliary Squadron. He was the first winner of the Forced Landing Trophy in 1929. Many members of the above Squadron, which served with distinction during the war, had their initial training with the Club under the guidance of 'Jock' Houston, who became the Chief Instructor in the early thirties. We shall always remember Squadron Leader Archie McKellar, who lost his life in the Battle of Britain, (sic) and who was decorated several times. It will be remembered how, flying with another member, George Pinkerton, they brought down some of the raiders on the Forth Bridge in the early days of the war (16th October 1939). Then there was 'Gibby' Rae, who started as an engineer apprentice with Northern and Scottish Airways, and eventually obtained his 'B' licence and flew for the same company. During the war, he was flying with British Overseas Airways Corporation and lost his life whilst on the Leuchars — Stockholm service. On two occasions, he was intercepted by enemy aircraft but managed to land his Mosquito safely.

Mention could be made of many Club pupils, who later served in one of the flying Services during the war with distinction, not a few of whom paid the supreme sacrifice. It has been stated by the Air Council, that Flying Clubs contribution to the war effort was negligible. It is difficult to reconcile this statement, when the record of the Scottish Flying Club alone, is considered.

AIRCRAFT OF THE SCOTTISH FLYING CLUB

1927-1956

1927-1939

G-EBUU D.H. 60X Moth. First aircraft, crashed Renfrew 1/5/28 (remains formed landing 'T' at Renfrew).

G-EBVT D.H. 60X Moth. Crashed Lumloch Colliery, near Glasgow, 10/2/29.

G-EBIQ D.H. 51 belonging to Air Comm. J. G. Weir, first flight 27/3/25 used by Scottish Flying Club in 1928.

G-AAFY D.H. 60G Moth to South Africa 0/37.

G-AAIU D.H. 60B Moth withdrawn from use 2/39.

G-AAJL D.H. 60G Moth impressed 18/2/41 as DG657.

G-ABAL D.H. 60G Moth bought June 1930.

the last four above replaced by

G-ABZS D.H. 60G III Moth impressed 23/8/40 as BD177

G-ABZT D.H. 60G III Moth crashed Islay 24/5/36.

G-ABZU D.H. 60G III Moth impressed 23/8/40 as BD178.

G-ABZV D.H. 60G III Moth impressed 23/8/40 as BD179.

They were delivered October, 1932

G-ACIB D.H. 60G III Moth impressed 23/8/40 as BD 175. Arr. Renfrew 4/8/3?

G-ACJB D.H. 60G III Moth noted in Scottish Flyer 9/37 ex. Miss J. M. Barbour.

G-ACDV D.H. 60G III Moth ex. T. G. Bishop.

G-AAZO D.H. 80A Puss Moth impressed 23/7/40 as AX870. Arr. Renfrew 8/5/32.

G-ACKL D.H. 85 Leopard Moth taken over from Major J. B. Watson about October, 1935.

G-ADML D.H. 87 Hornet Moth in service early 1936 after delivery delays.

G-ADKP D.H. 87 Hornet Moth noted 4/37 'green Hornet Moth' (S/F).

G-AEJK BAC Drone. Order noted for 'two BAC Super Drones' in Scottish Flyer, March 1936.

G-AEKM BAC Drone. ('de luxe drone/). Arrived February 1937 (S/F).

G-AAWZ Spartan Arrow — originally owned by John Sword.

G-AFJM D.H. 82A Tiger Moth impressed as BD170 late 1938.

G-AFJN D.H. 82A Tiger Moth impressed as BD171, flew with Glasgow University Air Squadron subsequently.

the last three bought in for Civil Air Guard Scheme

S/F — reported in 'Scottish Flyer'.

Statistics are given later in this history, which speak for themselves.

The Club had many first class women pilots, and it will not be out of place to mention a few and what they accomplished.

Miss Winifred Drinkwater (now Mrs. Short of flying-boat fame) was an outstanding pupil and won several trophies in various competitions. Miss J. Waters (now Mrs. S. Scott) won the forced landing competition in 1938, also the trophy for being the best woman pupil during the same year. Miss Margaret Cunnison was a very apt pupil, who gained her 'A' licence. She later had an instructors' course and became an instructor with the Strathtay Aero Club. During the war, she served with the Air Transport Auxiliary. Miss E. McDougall also flew with ATA and was a sound pilot. The Hon. Mrs. M. Fairweather became an instructor with the Club after the Civil Air Guard was formed and later joined ATA. She lost her life a month after her husband, Mr. Douglas Fairweather — a Club pupil — was killed whilst with ATA. Then there was Dr. Elizabeth Cook, who was unfortunately killed at Heston, when bound for the continent with Mrs. Fairweather in 1938. These are a few women pilots who were trained to fly by the Scottish Flying Club.

The Club sustained a great loss when the C.F.I. 'Jock' Houston was killed on 3rd July 1937, whilst a passenger in a Vega Gull G-AEWP, which was being demonstrated. He was a first-class instructor and was admired and respected by all his pupils. His successor was 'Sandy' Wren, an ex-Royal Flying Corps pilot, who carried on the tradition of the Club in turning out good pilots. He was an instructor at Perth during the war for some time.

The Scottish Flying Club was not only renowned for teaching men and women to fly, but it also had a great reputation for carrying out repairs and overhauls under the supervision of the Chief Engineer, Mr. Hugh Train. Work was done on aircraft and engines owned by Northern and Scottish Airways Ltd., the Edinburgh Flying Club, Strathtay Aero Club, Allied Airways Ltd. and the Carlisle Club. A very high standard of work was maintained. The majority of the engineering staff served with the Royal Air Force.

When the Civil Air Guard was launched in 1938, the Scottish Flying Club accepted the scheme and dealt with hundreds of applications from men and women who were anxious to learn to fly. Every applicant was interviewed and the most promising accepted. The Club bought two Tiger Moths, increased its paid instructors to four, in addition to four Honorary Instructors. A spacious and well furnished Clubroom was converted from a store, where meals and refreshments were obtainable. Lectures were held weekly, and everything possible done to ensure efficiency. Several times the Unit was inspected by Senior R.A.F. Officers, who spoke very highly of the smartness of the members. The Unit leader, Mr. M. Dryborough, who obtained his 'A' licence was not accepted by the R.A.F., so he joined the army and gained commission rank. On the outbreak of hostilities, all Club and private flying was banned. It is difficult to know why the C.A.G. was not allowed to continue its good work, as one of the reasons it was formed, was to create a reserve of pilots.

During the twelve months the scheme was operated, the Club trained 74 pilots who gained 'A' licences, whilst a further 120 were under instruction. Of the 74, eight served as pilots in the R.A.F., two in the R.N.A.S. and one in ATA; 12 were on aircrew duty with the R.A.F. The two in the R.N.A.S. were turned down by the R.A.F., but were accepted by the Admiralty and given commissioned rank immediately. One of them was awarded the D.S.C. and the other the D.F.C. All C.A.G. members could become members of the Scottish Flying Club on payment of the appropriate subscriptions.

On 1st September, 1939, when war was imminent, Renfrew Aerodrome was requisitioned from the Scottish Flying Club by the Air Ministry. As the lease with the Renfrew Town Council had been renewed in 1938 for a further five years, the Club was allowed to stay on the aerodrome and acted as caterers to personnel on the aerodrome. The Club aircraft were impounded by the R.A.F. and the engineering workshops had to close down. Members were not permitted to enter the aerodrome or to use the Clubrooms. On September 3rd, Messrs. Airwork General Trading Co. Ltd. were moved from Heston to Renfrew en bloc and took possession of the C.A.G. Clubroom and the four-bay hangar. Things generally were in a state of chaos for several weeks, but eventually some sort of order was established. The office staff of the Club were taken over by the Air Ministry and the Secretary (R.F. Millen) appointed Airport Manager. It was not long before drastic alterations took place to the Club premises. The first room to go was the lounge, which was turned into offices for Airwork. Later these offices were used by M.C.A. and British European Airways.

In November, 1940, No.309 Polish Squadron came to Renfrew which caused another upheaval. The Dining Room and Smokeroom formed the Officers' Mess and part of the sleeping quarters was turned into offices. The Club acted as caterers for the Squadron until May, 1941, when it left Renfrew. More accommodation was taken from the Club, until eventually, it was left with only the Dining Room and a portion of the Smokeroom, with much reduced sleeping accommodation.

The buildings suffered some damage during the raids on Clydeside and a 2,000 lb. bomb landed close to the four-bay hangar, but did not explode. Five years later it was removed from a depth of 20 ft. and caused quite a stir, as everybody had to be evacuated from the airport.

It has been stated that the Club had 210 pilot members at the oubreak of war. Of these, 44 served in the R.A.F. as pilots, three in the R.N.A.S. as pilots, and eight in ATA. Four instructors were instructing in the R.A.F. and 12 members were on ground duties with the R.A.F. As to casualties, 18 pilot members were killed in the R.A.F.

Decorations earned were as follows:- two OBEs; one MBE; one DSO; one DSC; four DFCs; and seven AFCs. Over a quarter of the Club's pilot members served in one or other of the flying services, and yet in spite of this wonderful record of which the Scottish Flying Club is justly proud, we are told that

Flying Clubs did not contribute very much towards the war effort. Whilst it is not possible to give any precise information regarding other Flying Clubs, there is no doubt that they all played their part in as much as their members were in one of the Services. It should be noted that our records are by no means complete, for, because of staff changes, an up-to-date register was not kept after 1943. There were also many members who served with the Army and Navy.

On April 1st, 1946, Civil Aviation was nationalised and Renfrew became a State Airport, now that it had two runways, which had been laid down during the war. It had been hoped that the Club would have been permitted to resume its activities at Renfrew, especially as it had been allowed to renew the lease on a yearly basis after the expiration in 1943. It soon became obvious, however, that any hope of returning to its old home was doomed, for in October, 1946, the Club received notice to quit in May, 1947. This was a hard blow, after all the money, time and energy which had been spent during the pre-war years in encouraging aviation in Scotland, not to mention the fact that the Scottish Flying Club had earned for itself, a remarkable reputation in the flying world, and built up a Club which was considered to be the finest in the country. On May 28th, 1947, the Club relinquished what little hold it had on Renfrew Airport, including all its premises, for which no compensation was payable. This was because the Club was permitted to run the full term of the lease, which made the compensation clause in-operative. The Club was allowed to retain an office at the airport, which by the irony of fate, is the same one it occupied in 1927. In 1948 the Club was practically back at its starting point, except that it had a great deal of experience and tradition behind it. It also had some aircraft, a good membership, a little capital, and a very keen committee, but what it wanted more than anything else was an aerodrome. A great deal of time was spent in searching for a site within easy reach of Glasgow, but without success. Several sites were inspected, but found to be useless.

In 1947, His Grace the Duke of Hamilton, who was an enthusiastic member, very generously offered the Club, 192 acres, part of which, it was considered would make an ideal site for Club flying. It was inspected, and although not exactly like a billiard table, it appeared to be suitable after a certain amount of work had been done to the surface. The Agricultural War Executive were approached to see if there were any objections to making an aerodrome on the site, and informed the club that it could go ahead. The Town and Country Planning Department were then consulted, and after four months delay, stated that there were no objections. Then came the stumbling block in the shape of the Ministry of Civil Aviation. On making application for a licence, the Club was faced with a schedule of requirements to be made out first. Gone were the old days, when it was only necessary for a 'B' licence pilot to make a few landings on a site, and then sign on the dotted line, to obtain a licence.

The new requirements called for two stripways, 500 yards long and 100 yards wide, 60 degrees apart, with provision for a third stripway. The overall gradient had not to exceed 1 in 60, and local gradients not more than 1 in 40 for 300 feet. In addition, the Club had to state how many man hours would be required by engineers, labourers, vehicles, etc. before a licence could be obtained to carry out the work. The Club employed a firm of Civil Engineers to survey the site and give an estimate for the work to be done to meet these requirements. It was no less that £9,000, and that merely to put the ground in order. A fair sized hangar was reckoned to cost £4,500, plus a further £4,500 to lay a concrete floor. There still remained clubrooms and offices to be provided at an estimated cost of £3,500, making a total estimated cost of £22,000, before flying could start. On top of this there was the cost to buy fire-fighting equipment and all the other odds and ends to satisfy the M.C.A. Obviously this was beyond the financial resources of the Club, so it was with reluctance that the Club had to terminate negotiations with the Duke of Hamilton.

Hearing of the Club's desperate position, Airwork Ltd., who owned Perth Aerodrome, suggested that the Scottish Flying Club should operate from Perth on a contract basis at a set figure for dual and solo flying, and that all Scottish Flying Club members should become Honorary Members of Airwork Club, which was also used by the Strathtay Aero Club.

The Committee agreed to this suggestion, and lost no time in getting two of six Australian built Tiger Moths, which had previously been obtained, into the air. Thus it was that the Club started to fly again in August, 1947. The members were charged the same rates which were paid to Airwork. Consequently there was no profit on flying, but a loss, as the Club paid for insurance on the aircraft, and the cost to assemble and obtain British Certificate of Airworthiness was far beyond that expected. Travelling curtailed the activities of the Club and as there was little to offer members, the Annual Subscriptions were considerably reduced, and were ten shillings per annum for Associates, and £1 per annum for Pilot Members. The Entrance Fee was also waived.

It was thought that if a centre could be found in Glasgow, where members could meet and have meals, it would assist in an interest being maintained, but as soon as we came upon a likely building, it was either the cost to buy, or some government regulation which prevented the Club from going ahead. No matter which way the Club turned, it was barred by rules, regulations and prohibitions laid down by the powers that be.

On 10th December 1947, the Scottish Flying Club celebrated its Twenty-First Anniversary by having a dinner dance at the Central Hotel, Glasgow, when over 300 were present.

*   *   *

The post-war story of the Scottish Flying Club was not a happy one. Reginald Millen has detailed some of the problems which the Club experienced before starting operations at Scone. Three of the six Tiger Moths which had been bought from Australia, were eventually put into operation, G-AKCG, G-AKCH and G-AKCI, not all at one time however. Two of the rest, G-AKYL, and G-AKYM were sold abroad in 1950, while investigations and negotiations for a more convenient flying site continued. A proposal to buy an Auster, suitable for use at Renfrew was considered, costs were put at £2.15s.0d. and £3.0s.0d. per hour — nothing came of it.

Prominent among the post-war Committee of the Club were Frank Mickel, the builder; John McKean, the butcher; and George Pinkerton, the farmer; Col. McWilliam, motor dealer; all pre-war members, and G.S. Meek, owner of two Moth Minors G-AFOB and G-AFRY which were to be seen at Renfrew in the early 1950s, along with N.B. Ewing's Auster 5 G-AKPH.

In 1950, the Air Ministry produced a scheme to give flying training to air cadets. To its credit, the scheme also had the intention of assisting the struggling post-war flying club movement. This spurred on the Scottish Flying Club, and negotiations with Prestwick's Commandant, Jimmy Jeffs, and the MCA's Scottish Deputy Controller, Donaldson were pursued. The latter flew a Taylorcraft Plus D, G-AHUG, based for a time at Prestwick, and which he offered to the Scottish Flying Club for their use at 35/- per hour. It was also noted that ex-RAF Tiger Moths were to become available at £20.0s.0d. each! Curiously, just as permission to operate from Prestwick appeared to be assured, the Club were refused — due, it would seem to protests from BOAC. Given the low frequency of operations there and indeed at Renfrew, it is difficult to understand these objections — there is no great problem for the Glasgow Flying Club, the West of Scotland Flying Club, and the Universities Air Squadron, operating from the new Glasgow Airport. Grangemouth was also a serious contender in 1950/51. However, its days were numbered as the local authority needed the land for housing — Balado and Turnberry, even Abbotsinch were considered — to no avail.

Eventually, with support from Glasgow Chamber of Commerce and others, an approach was made to the Government Minister responsible, who also happened to be MP for West Renfrewshire, Mr. J.S. Maclay, MP (later Lord Muirshiel). The Club was allowed to return to Renfrew with various conditions. Its tenacity being finally rewarded by the granting of official permission in March, 1952 — more travail awaited them however. They were not able to return to the splendid Club premises they built in 1934, which had since become Renfrew's civil terminal.

Miles Magisters, Hawk Trainer IIIs in civilian guise, were bought and fitted with the required radio equipment and brakes by Airwork at Perth, under the ever helpful Wing Commander Nugent. Mr. W.E. Bradley was appointed C.F.I.

Of the three Tigers which had been made airworthy at Perth, 'KCG had been sold abroad, 'KCH was sold to the Strathtay Club at Perth for £200 in August, 1952, and 'KCI was ferried to Renfrew at the expiry of its C & A in June 1952, awaiting sale. In September of that year, Magister G-AJRV, first in operation, had been damaged in a ground loop, however, the Club was lucky in obtaining the part-time services of two British European Airways' engineers, Messrs. Hunter and McEwan at 4/- per hour, and by the end of the year, Magisters G-AHKP, G-AJHG, G-AKKS and G-AKKY had been purchased though there were difficulties in getting them radio equipped for service at Renfrew and generally maintaining them. They did not prove to be a good buy. For instance, in June, 1953, only 'HKP and 'KKY were servicable, 'JHG and 'JRV, being under repair. At a Committee Meeting on 10th December, 1952, in Chairman, Frank Mickel's office at West George Street, Glasgow, the colours of the aircraft were discussed, with yellow and red being proposed and accepted. In fact not all the aircraft were so finished and the Miles Messenger G-AJDF which was bought in the summer of 1953, was painted a light blue all over, with dark blue letters.

The Club was officially visited in September, 1953, by Flt. Lt. Whyte of RAF Home Command, who gave it a very satsifactory report in connection with the training of cadets. It is interesting to note that in March, 1954, the real cost of flying (not the lower figure actually charged), was with overheads, worked out at £7.7s.2d. per hour — the author recalls paying £7.10s.0d. per hour in 1969. In fact the cost of private flying has always been high, even in the thirties, the hourly rate was about equivalent to the weekly wage of a skilled worker in the shipyards. Clearly the Club had to use its capital to subsidise its flying operations at Renfrew, which, taken with the maintenance problems of the aircraft, and difficulties in obtaining the services of part-time instructors, made the Club's position perilous. Would the purchase of a Chipmunk help, at £740 , plus the cost of civil conversion? — No. The situation which the Scottish Flying Club found itself in was common enough then and still is with flying clubs and groups in the UK, due to the high costs of flying, some of which result from the needs and attitudes of officialdom. Typical deficits were reported at the Club's 26th Annual General Meeting held in the Central Hotel, Glasgow, on Wednesday, 24th November, 1954 — minus £977.12s.2d. in the flying account and minus £587.16s.9d. on the ground. Even when better accommodation was granted to the Club at Renfrew, the kind of revenue which the bar and other social activities required to subsidise the flying, could not be generated.

It was noted at a committee meeting about then, that Cadet Rosenbloom had reported for training on 21st November. Capt. Geoff. Rosenbloom, whose flying career included service with the RAF's crack 43 (Fighter) Squadron, became one of Loganair's original pilots and in 1990, was still very active in the charter field at Glasgow Airport.

A further RAF Home Command inspection in May, 1955, found them impressed with the Scottish Flying Club's organisation. Two further Magisters had been bought, G-AJDR and G-ALIM, and consideration was given to the purchase of an Auster Aiglet. Sadly, on 29th September, 1955, F.J. Osborne, a recently joined member from the South was killed in the Magister G-AJRV in a crash near Alexandria. G-AHKP had previously forced-landed on the Greenock Golf Course on 4th August, 1954, and G-AJHG had also been written off near Glasgow, on 22nd June, 1954 — neither case resulting in fatalities.

At the 1954 Annual General Meeting on 8th October, in the Clubrooms at Renfrew, flying hours for the past year were reported as 605, down on the previous year's 710. Four new PPLs had been achieved and one cadet had qualified. Despite much effort, there was a lamentable lack of cadet candidates in the West of Scotland. The Chairman, Frank Mickel commented that he would like to see 'a twin, such as Rapide in our hangar' — what there was, were Magisters G-AKKY, G-ALIM and G-AJDR, with the Messenger G-AJDF. A loss of £2,318.5s.6d. in cash reserves was reported, as were substantial increases in hangar rents. In January, 1956, the future of the Scottish Flying club was being earnestly debated. The eventual result, agreed at an Extraordinary Annual General Meeting on 10th March, 1956, being the decision to form a new Club at Perth, from the Scottish Flying Club and the Strathtay Aero Club. It was to be known as the Scottish Aero Club. The shrewd George Pinkerton ensured that the Scottish Flying Club's capital was conserved and indeed the Club, as a limited company, would continue until its final dissolution in 1979. The new Club's vice-chairman was the Scottish Flying Club's, Frank Mickel, and their remaining aircraft, Magisters G-AJDR and G-ALIM together with the Messenger G-AJDF were due to be flown to Perth on Sunday, 25th March — weather permitting. Magister, G-AKKY, had suffered an accident and was under repair, so joined the new Club later on.

The Scottish Flying Club did continue to function as a source of support for popular flying in the West of Scotland. By the end of 1961, the Scottish Aero Club had radically changed its way of working, no longer owning its aircraft, rather chartering them from Airwork, the owners and operators at Scone, from where they were still operating in 1990.

One of the Scottish Flying Club's members, Dr. Frank Roche, had become a leading light in the Rutherglen group of the Popular Flying Association. They had built their own aircraft, a Turbi, G-APBO, in the late 1950s. They sought help from the Scottish Flying Club regarding the purchase of Couplaw Farm, Strathaven, for use as a flying field. The Club did, in fact, purchase the farm, allowing its use to various organisations for both power flying and gliding, including the West of Scotland Flying Club and the Clydesdale Flying Club. One of the groups flying there in the 1960s bought an Auster which, among other problems, shed its propeller one day, luckily without injury. Gliding was established at Couplaw by the Glasgow Universities' Gliding Club, which expanded into the Universities' Gliding Club.

At the Annual General Meeting of the Scottish Flying Club at 91 West George Street, on Monday, 9th February, 1976, with George Pinkerton in the Chair, it was proposed that the Club be finally wound up, with the remaining assets to be divided between the RAF Benevolent Fund and Erskine Hospital. It took some time for the legal and other formalities to be completed, indeed the Club did not cease to exist until after the general meeting of members held at 2 West Regent Street, Glasgow, on Wednesday, 25th July, 1979. The land at Couplaw Farm was donated to the RAF Benevolent Fund, who have continued to allow its use for flying and gliding. £1,000 also went to Linburn Hospital for the war blinded, and the balance of funds to Erskine Hospital. Group Captain George Pinkerton, OBE, DFC, the Club's last Chairman, relinquished office after an association with it of almost fifty years.

D.H.60GIII Moth, G-ABVW, flown into 5th place, King's Cup Race, by H.S. Broad, 1932, at astonishing speed (for Moths) of 131-134 mph. Sold to Amy Johnson, who named it 'Jason 4'. Following her marriage to Jim Mollison on 29th July, 1932, she flew it from Stag Lane to Renfrew for a Scottish honeymoon.

G-ACAB, D.H.80A Puss Moth. 'Desert Cloud', flown by Amy Mollison, when she beat her husband's Cape record by 10 hrs. 26 mins. — she broke that record on return!

D.H.80A, single-seater. G-ABKG, flown by Jim Mollison from Lympne to Cape in 4 days 17 hrs. 19 mins. leaving on 24th March, 1932.

S.M.T. Fox Moth, one of the first two, in Hillman's Airways colours, 1932.

The Scottish Motor Traction Co.'s aviation division main base was at Renfrew from July, 1932. Seen there are their three Dragons with two of their eight Fox Moths, G-ACEJ and G-ACED, and one of their Avro Club Cadets, G-ACFH are seen. S.M.T. moved to the East in the Autumn of 1933. G-ACEJ, together with one of Midland & Scottish Air Ferries Ltd.'s Fox Moths, G-ACCB, was sold to Norman Giroux in 1936 for pleasure flying from Birkdale Sands, Southport — they were still at it in the 1960's. Both, or their remains were under restoration/rebuild in 1990.

P I O N E E R I N G

P R O G R E S S

Positive identification from 200 feet up!

R.H. Soundy, Pilot, S.M.T. Aviation Department, 1933/34.

←

This photograph which was taken circa mid-1933, shows G-ACEJ, with a cockpit canopy — it must have been removed, subsequently.

THE economic depression of the early 1930s was indeed a pretty dismal time for the country as a whole and certainly for Glasgow and Clydeside.

Against this unencouraging background, a few hardy souls were pursuing their visions of revolutionising the difficult transport links around the Islands and North of Scotland by the introduction of regular services by aeroplane. E.E. Fresson at Inverness, had been active since 1929, E.L. Gandar-Dower was at Aberdeen and the man who was to be first in establishing regular air services in Scotland, John Sword was at Renfrew!

The Scottish Flying Club had begun to encourage public awareness of aviation and in May, 1929, had arranged a visit, not perhaps her first, to Renfrew by the Imperial Airways, Armstrong Whitworth Argosy G-EBLF *City of Glasgow*. She was captained by the legendary O.P. Jones and was opened to the public. Incidentally, this aircraft was used in the race between an express train, the LNER's *Flying Scotsman* and an airliner, from London (Croydon) to Edinburgh (Turnhouse) on June 15th, 1928. The Argosy won by 15 minutes, having had to stop twice to refuel. Also during 1930, what must have been the precursor to the Scottish Air Ambulance Service took place. This was the delivery to Islay of urgently needed medical supplies by air through the good offices of Flying Officers Lloyd and Powell of the resident 602 Squadron. Winifred Drinkwater, a lady who would soon become famous, received her private 'A' flying licence at the Scottish Flying Club in August of 1930, and the Club was visited by another famous aviatrix, Amy Johnson. She was soon to marry another record-breaking flyer, Jim Mollison, from Glasgow.

Fresson had been surveying possible routes from Inverness and Gandar-Dower likewise from Aberdeen. However, it was John Sword, a bus operator from Airdrie, who, having combined his business , the Midland Bus Co., with the Scottish Motor Traction Co. in Edinburgh, began planning the first truly regular air services in Scotland. He encouraged his fellow Directors in S.M.T. to form an aviation division which began charter operations in July, 1932. It was initially based at Renfrew and then, from the Autumn of 1933, over at Macmerry. However, what was forming in John Sword's mind was a far greater vision — the creation of a network of scheduled services serving not only the remoter Western Isles of Scotland, but creating trunk routes the length of the country. Indeed, by connecting up with Hillman's Airways at Romford Essex, Glasgow (Renfrew) was to be connected to Paris — 'breakfast in Glasgow, afternoon tea in Paris'.

Amongst other pressing matters in 1931, the Government began encouraging local authorities to paint the town's name on their gasometers — surely one of the first navigational aids after road signs — Greenock was amongst the first to comply! In 1920, names had been painted on railway stations as an aid to aerial navigation!

In June, 1931, the Scottish Flying Club held what was becoming their annual aerial pageant at Renfrew. These three-day events were hugely popular with attendances of around 100 000. Joy riding was a great feature. After all, few people would have had the chance to fly. On one occasion, over 10 000 people flew with over 100 aircraft performing. Barnard's Air Circus visited during August, 1931, and Sir Alan Cobham's National Aviation Days display, the following month. With Barnard's was Jim Mollison and the Scottish Flying Club duly entertained him at dinner in the Central Hotel, Glasgow. Mollison, born in Glasgow, achieved fame by his record breaking flights, including the first solo Atlantic crossing East to West. He married Amy Johnson in July, 1932, and they began their honeymoon from Renfrew — a marriage which sadly, didn't last.

However, 1932 must be regarded as the year in which Scottish Civil Aviation really came of age, when many of the routes which are still being flown nearly sixty years later, were being planned. At the Scottish Flying Club, Renfrew, Winnie Drinkwater achieved a 'B' licence, making her at 19 years of age, probably the youngest female commercial pilot in the world. She had also achieved her instructor's rating and ground engineer's licence — the actual receipt of which had to await her 21st birthday.

John Sword was a real entrepreneur and a man of extensive vision, with multifarious enthusiasms. He was a big man in every sense. Throughout his life, his energy and talents brought him into contact with a whole cross-section of society, from bus drivers to belted Earls, yet he didn't forget his humbler beginnings in the Burgh of Airdrie, within industrial Lanarkshire, where he was born on 17th April, 1892.

His family had the Groveside Bakery business in the town, and from an early interest in the horses, which provided the transport, he developed, during his time as a motor transport officer in the Royal Flying Corps., a fascination for motor vehicles. This eventually led to the formation of Midland Bus Services at Airdrie. The age of the motor bus had arrived and it was challenging the erstwhile dominance of the railways in the arena of public transport — the railway companies would soon fight back, as will be seen. John Sword, in many ways, made Renfrew airport.

In the east, the Scottish Motor Traction Co. under Sir William Thomson, Lord Provost of Edinburgh, had become a major bus operator. In 1929, Midland Bus Services was sold to SMT with John Sword becoming a Director and Manager of Western SMT, based at Kilmarnock in 1932. An interest in flying had been kindled during his war service, which, when coupled to his war time experience in motor transport had fired his imagination, and encouraged him to persuade SMT's board to establish an Aviation Department. The summer of 1932 saw this in being at Renfrew under its Commercial Manager, M.R. Beveridge; Air Superintendent, Flt. Lt. N.M.S. Russell; and Chief Pilot, Sqn. Ldr. H.G.R. Malet, the latter collecting the first aircraft, de Havilland Fox Moth G-ABWB, on 2nd July, from Edward Hillman at Romford. Hillman was a fellow bus operator from the east-end of London, similarly fired by the promise of air-transport and Sword enjoyed a productive relationship with

One of S.M.T.'s D.H.84 Dragons, G-ACET, in their silver and blue colour scheme. The S.M.T. badge had gold lettering on, what must be assumed, a blue background, outlined in black. This aircraft was also being rebuilt in 1990.

SFC Air Pageant 15th, 16th June 1935 'Bill Kingwill's' Avros.

Sir Alan Cobham's National Aviation Day display, Renfrew.

49

him, beginning by his taking two Fox Moths originally ordered by Hillman. The second aircraft, G-ABWF, was delivered the next day and immediately began commercial operations, giving joy-rides around Edinburgh — joy-riding by 'plane, being a popular activity in those times. Later on SMT was to be the first to land an aircraft on Shetland.

The railways, meanwhile, had been taking an increasing interest in the bus companies for their mutual benefit, and, on the board of SMT, the LMS Railway Co. had a powerful voice. They were already making plans for their own air services, perhaps provoked by Sword's emerging ideas, and SMT's flying activities which, however, never went beyond joy-riding and charters.

In the autumn of 1932, John Sword, from his Kilmarnock base, was laying the plans for his own airline company. He could see the unique advantages of direct air transport to the island communities of Scotland, and to those which, because of the indented nature of the topography, were a long way by road and a slow way by sea. He also had an even more extensive plan which would include the whole of the UK and connect to Europe.

Thus, was Midland & Scottish Air Ferries born — Midland from his old bus company and Air Ferries, not only for its obvious description of what he was proposing to do, but also after his first aircraft, Airspeed Ferry G-ACBT, bought from the makers new, for £3,975 less £900 given for his Bentley 6.5 litre car, taken in part exchange! This aircraft was to be delivered on the 8th of February, 1933, along with his second, Fox Moth G-ACBZ. Unfortunately, G-ACBT was damaged during the flight on landing en route at Edinburgh, leaving the Fox Moth to attend the arrival ceremony at Renfrew. During early 1933, SMT announced a great expansion of its aviation activities licencing no less than 64 aerodromes in Scotland and building up its fleet to 16 aircraft, including twin-engined D.H.84 Dragons, really a twin Fox Moth, more of the latter, Avro Cadets and a Tiger Moth. Meanwhile Midland & Scottish Air Ferries began building up their fleet. Another Fox Moth, G-ACCB, arrived on 10th February — she was to have a remarkably long life, for after serving Midland & Scottish Air Ferries, spending many years with Giro Aviation, joy-riding from the beach at Southport until in 1956, she force-landed into the sea.

With the opening of the 1933 British Industries Fair at Castle Bromwich near Birmingham, the fledgling airline operated a scheduled air taxi service between Liverpool (Speke), Hooton Park (Cheshire) and Castle Bromwich, from 20th February until 2nd March — under contract to the aircraft dealers, Brian Lewis & Co. At Renfrew, events which were to have even greater moments thirty years later, were taking place. 602 Squadron, having found the Moorpark airfield too cramped for their operations, moved over to the new base at Abbotsinch. With the ending of the Air Ministry's lease of Renfrew, shortly thereafter, the Town Council concluded a new lease of the now officially named Renfrew Aerodrome with the Scottish Flying Club, by now a substantial organisation. The SFC was also to act as the Aerodrome Managers, and one of Chief Instructor, John Houston's star pupils, Winnie Drinkwater, having achieved her 'B' commercial flying licence, was taken on by John Sword in March, 1933, as one of his new pilots. Since she was also a qualified ground

	Aircraft		Engines		Journey		Time of Departure		Time of Arrival		Time in Air		Pilot	Remarks
Date.	Type.	Markings.	Type.	H.P.	From.	To.	Hrs.	Mins.	Hrs.	Mins.	Hrs.	Mins.	See Instructions (5) & (6) on flyleaf of this book.	
						Brought forward	...	...	...	...	779	30		
20.6.34	WR0642	GACIH	Genet	140	Renfrew	Sphere Hendon					4	00	Self	For Lord Londonderry
21.6.34	DH83	GACCU	Gipsy	130	"	Sphere retn					1	10	"	Charter
23.6.34	"	"	"	"	"	Local						10	"	Engine test
25.6.34	"	"	"	"	"	Sphere return Sphere Blackfoot return					4	30	"	Airline
27.6.34	"	"	"	"							4	30	"	"
4.7.34	"	B2	"	"	Renfrew Sphere London Sphere Renfrew						8	30	"	"
5.7.34	"	"	"	"	Renfrew Hull Renfrew						5	00	"	Charter
											808	20		
						Carried forward	...	...	...	...				

Renfrew, 1933/34.
Jimmy Orrell, John Rae and Winnie Drinkwater — pilots, with Mary Drinkwater (behind Winnie), Midland & Scottish Air Ferries secretary.

engineer and flying instructor, in this, as in so many other things, Sword got full value! Winnie was likely to be the youngest, female commercial pilot in the world then. He also had just employed John Rae, from de Havillands as Chief Pilot at Renfrew, Malet being Midland & Scottish Air Ferries' Chief Pilot, and in April, Jimmy Orrell was recruited. He became famous as Chief Test Pilot for Avro at Manchester.

The build-up of John Sword's airline proceeded apace and on 18th April, its first scheduled service was inaugurated — effectively Renfrew's and Scotland's first as well. It was to Campbeltown, and operated in collaboration with the *Scottish Daily Express*, allowing the speedy delivery of their newspapers. Two Fox Moths flew the inaugural services that day, G-ACCT flown by Jimmy Orrell and G-ACCU flown by John Rae. They arrived at the Strath airfield at around 7 o' clock in the morning! Like many of the early pioneers' services in Scotland, it was still being flown nearly sixty years later — Sword, together with Fresson at Inverness, and Gandar Dower at Aberdeen, got it right!

On 20th April, the Campbeltown service was extended to Islay, with John Rae flying Fox Moth, G-ACCU, anticipating the start of regular services on 16th May. A week later, Winnie Drinkwater, performed her first scheduled trip on the Renfrew — Campbeltown route in the Fox Moth, G-ACBZ — the first Scottish scheduled flight commanded by a woman.

John Sword made many significant friendships during his life — one being with Roy, later Sir Roy Dobson of Avros at Manchester, and it was from him that he bought, not only the two-seat Cadets, of which SMT also had a fleet, but an Avro Ten airliner the Type 618, a three-engined, high wing monoplane of Fokker lineage. This aircraft, G-ACGF, Midland & Scottish Air Ferries' eighth arrived at Renfrew on 5th May, allowing Jimmy Orrell to inaugurate a Renfrew to Belfast (Aldergrove) service on the 30th. Ed Stewart in the Dragon, C-ACCZ, also flew to Aldergrove that day via Campbeltown.

Truly significant though the inauguration of these services were, Jimmy Orrell's flight on 14th May stands out on its own, for it was the very first official air ambulance charter. He flew the Dragon G-ACCZ, from Renfrew to Loch Indaal on Islay to pick up John McDermid, a fisherman, seriously ill with peritonitis. A Glasgow nurse, Mrs A.W. Ferguson, who happened to be on the island accompanied him on the flight back to Renfrew and, on arrival, he was rushed to the nearby Southern General Hospital where, after surgery, he thankfully recovered. The aeroplane had become an instrument of humanitarian purpose — at Renfrew by John Sword. The flying nurses of the

Southern General are still performing their errands of mercy — after completing ten operational flights, each nurse receives a pair of Silver Wings.

Sword's ideas were now becoming realities. He was surveying potential routes to the Western Isles and including Rothesay in the Campbeltown service, and on 7th July, Midland & Scottish Air Ferries' pilot, Noel Mavrogordato, landed on a field at Monkton near Prestwick in Fox Moth G-ACBZ. It came into more regular use by Midland & Scottish Air Ferries and, developed by that other great visionary, David McIntyre, became Prestwick International Airport, and from 1935, the home of Scottish Aviation Ltd. It seems that John Sword had sought Jimmy Jeffs from Croydon's advice on a suitable site in the area and that it was he, who had made the choice of the Monkton site. Jimmy Jeffs was to become a 'weel kent' Commandant of Prestwick, post-war. The nearby Orangefield Hotel began advertising its attractiveness to aviators. In these days, there were very few aerodromes and pilots merely sought suitable fields with agreeable landowners. Renfrew in the mid-1930s was the second municipal aerodrome in the UK, becoming an *airport* on 30th April, 1934, with the provision of full Customs' facilities — necessary for such services as those to Eire.

Developments at Midland & Scottish Air Ferries were not restricted to Scotland, as on 16th July, Sword officially inspected the new base at Hooton Park, Cheshire — an important link in the growing chain. Indeed, he was establishing the 'hub' concept much in vogue fifty and more years later. Midland & Scottish Air Ferries had, by the end of August, 1933, established a number of routes from Liverpool to the Isle of Man, via Blackpool and to Dublin. The Isle of Man had begun to be served from Renfrew the previous month. Yet a further innovation at that time was the introduction of a stewardess, Mrs. Dorothy Sparkes, wife of 'Ned' Sparkes, one of Midland & Scottish Air Ferries' pilots at Renfrew. During the late autumn of 1933/34, some of the services were shut down for the winter, particularly those from the Hooton Park and Speke bases, and Sword announced reduced fares on its schedules from Renfrew.

The weather in the Clyde Valley has never been particularly kind to aviators, even after the Clean Air Act, and the closure of much of the area's heavy industry. November regularly brought fogs, real pea soupers and so it was in the first year of real airline operations from Renfrew. Midland & Scottish Air Ferries' services had to be 'diverted', indeed relocated to the fields at Monkton — Prestwick. Some Renfrew diversions also went to the RAF's Abbotsinch and Eric Starling recalled diverting there in October ,1934, with his Aberdeen Airways Dragon G-ACAN — later named the *Starling*. Abbotsinch's position, between the White and Black Cart rivers, made it easier to locate.

1933 was a remarkable year for Renfrew, yet John Sword had much greater plans. In January 1934 he announced that in March he intended to link the Western Isles and Ireland with the Continent, the plan being for Midland & Scottish Air Ferries to connect at Liverpool with his own services to Croydon and from there by Imperial Airways to Paris. In addition, Midland & Scottish Air Ferries also connected at Hull with KLM's Amsterdam service. However, it was on the 6th of April, 1934, that the ground plan was finally completed. At Liverpool's Speke Airport, at a ceremony where the Prime Minister, Ramsay MacDonald, named Midland & Scottish Air Ferries' latest aircraft, the Avro 642 G-ACFV *Marchioness of Londonderry*, in honour of the wife of the Air Minister, John Sword announced the start of new services between Liverpool and London, and in collaboration, with Hillman's Airways-Paris, which were, of course, to be related to the existing network of services to Belfast, Blackpool and the Isle of Man. On the 9th, London (Romford) — Liverpool — Glasgow (Renfrew) service began — the beginning of true airline services between Glasgow and London. The aircraft used were Fox Moth G-ACCB from Romford to Speke; Dragon G-ACDL from Speke to Romford; and at the Renfrew end, Fox Moths and Dragon G-ACDL together with the Avro ten, G-ACGF. Winnie Drinkwater flew the route on May, 25th and 26th in Fox Moth G-ACCU, being the first female pilot to do so. Thus, with great vision and energy, harnessed to business acumen, John Sword had created with his Midland & Scottish Air Ferries Ltd., a national carrier servicing the remoter communities in Scotland, and linking them with a trunk network connected onward to Europe. His was at once, a Scottish, a British and a European vision. It would be hardly surprising if he had now been talking to his friends in the aircraft industry about crossing the Atlantic.

Success, sadly causes resentment and envy, and there were those who had their own schemes for air travel, and who were not to be thwarted. The railway companies, their monopoly seriously challenged by the emerging bus operators had been buying their way into these new businesses and were awake to the further threat which the embryonic airlines could pose. On SMT's board, the dominant influence of Sir Josiah Stamp of the LMS railway was to be crucial. The railways began organising their own airline company in association with Imperial Airways, the state's chosen instrument. John Sword had demonstrably shown the way, but as SMT's Western Manager, he could not be allowed to continue. In June, the SMT board told him to either close his airline or leave SMT.

Given the colossal, personal investment of time, energy and money, which he had put into his airline which, though not yet profitable, would almost certainly have become so, it must have been an agonising decision for him. However, with whatever regrets, he decided to close down Midland & Scottish Air Ferries Ltd. by the end of September, 1934. The London and Liverpool services finished on July, 14th. An attempt to continue some sort of aviation activity at Blackpool's, Stanley Park airfield, came to nought. SMT had also wound up their flying affairs. Sword, however, kept the air ambulance service in being, until its future could be secured. Thus ended the practical realisation of John Sword's broad vision. He had created Scotland's first airline and in the short space of about two years, had built up an internal route network and a fleet of 17 aircraft, the largest until BEA was formed in 1946.

Early in 1934, Short Bros. brought the prototype Scion aircraft G-ACJI to Renfrew — it went on to Inverness and in its crew was Francis Short, a director of the firm. He met Winnie, and after a whirlwind romance, they

Winnie Drinkwater in front of Midland & Scottish Air Ferries' Avro Cadet.

Winnie Drinkwater and American boxing promotor at Renfrew with Midland & Scottish Air Ferries' de Havilland Dragon.

Winnie Drinkwater and John Houston.

Midland & Scottish Air Ferries' line-up at Renfrew c.1934. John Sword (second left) with Winnie and Mary Drinkwater on his left and right.

First scheduled air service in Scotland. Loading newspapers at Renfrew aerodrome for Campeltown and first freight flight, 8th April 1933. Left to right: Winnie Drinkwater, John Rae, Jimmy Orrell, Press employee, Mary Drinkwater, Press employee.

John Sword's personal Dragon, G-ACJS. (G-AC John Sword).

Midland & Scottish Air Ferries. Airspeed Ferry at Renfrew.
Back Row: Mary Drinkwater, Jimmy Orrell, I. MacDonald
Front Row: Winnie Drinkwater, John Rae

Opening of Midland & Scottish Air Ferries Renfrew to Islay service.

Midland & Scottish fleet at Renfrew, 1934

The first Scottish air ambulance flight — by D.H.84 Dragon, G-ACCZ, of Midland & Scottish Air Ferries to and from Renfrew, 14th May, 1933, pilot, Jimmy Orrell.

'The day of the great beast's arrival',
Avro Ten Type 6l8, G-ACGF.
L. to R. Mary Drinkwater, John Sword,
McDonald, Mr. ?, A. Jack (Engineer), A.
Drinkwater, H. Goldie.

'Official opening of M&SAF's new
London service, Speke — 6th/7th(?)
April, 1934'. Avro Type 642, G-ACFV.

The Renfrew Fire Service in the 1930s.

NORTHERN & SCOTTISH AIRWAYS LIMITED
Airport for Glasgow, Renfrew
PHONE: RENFREW 230

TIME TABLE FROM JULY FIRST TO OCTOBER SECOND

LINE 111.

RENFREW — CAMPBELTOWN — ISLAY.
1st July to 2nd October, except where otherwise stated.
Sundays excepted.

			a.m.	a.m.	p.m. A†	p.m. *	p.m.
GLASGOW	.. Grosvenor Restaurant	dep.	9-00	10-00	1-30	4-30	6-00
	..RENFREW AIRPORT	dep.	9-45	10-45	2-15	5-15	6-45
	..KINTYRE AIRPORT	arr.	10-30	11-30	..	..	7-30
CAMPBELTOWN..	White Hart Hotel	arr.	10-45	11-45	..	..	7-45
	.. White Hart Hotel	dep.	10-15	..	..	..	7-00
	..KINTYRE AIRPORT	dep.	10-35	..	..	..	7-35
	..GLENEGEDALE						
ISLAY	.. AIRPORT	arr.	11-00	..	3-05	6-05	8-00
	.. Port Ellen	arr.	..	..	..	..	..

ISLAY — CAMPBELTOWN — RENFREW.
1st July to 2nd October, except where otherwise stated.
Sundays excepted.

			a.m.	a.m.	a.m.	p.m. A†	p.m. *
ISLAY	.. Port Ellen ..	dep.	..	..	..	..	..
	..GLENEGEDALE						
	.. AIRPORT ..	dep.	8-15	..	11-40	4-0:	6-45
	..KINTYRE AIRPORT	arr.	8-40	..	..	..	7-10
CAMPBELTOWN..	White Hart Hotel	arr.	8-55	..	..	..	7-25
	.. White Hart Hotel	dep.	8-25	11-30	..	..	7-00
	..KINTYRE AIRPORT	dep.	8-45	11-45	..	..	7-15
GLASGOW	..RENFREW AIRPORT	arr.	9-30	12-30 (p.m.)	12-30 (p.m.)	4-50	8-00
	.. Grosvenor Restaurant	arr.	10-00	1-00	1-00	5-30	8-30

NOTES.—A—Friday, Saturday and Monday only.   * Operates one hour earlier from 1st September.   † Service discontinues 1st September.
GROUND TRANSPORT:— PROVIDED BY THE COMPANY AT GLASGOW AND CAMPBELTOWN: AT ISLAY CARS CAN BE OBTAINED AT PREFERRED RATES

LINE 222.

GLASGOW — ISLE OF MAN.
1st July to 2nd October, except where otherwise stated.
Daily unless otherwise stated.

			a.m. N.S. †	a.m.	p.m. C‡ SO	p.m. NS *
GLASGOW	.. Grosvenor Restaurant	dep.	9-00	10-00	3-00	6-00
	..RENFREW AIRPORT	dep.	9-40	10-45	3-45	6-45
	..HALL CAINE AIRPORT	arr.	10-55	12-00	5-00	8-00
ISLE OF MAN	.. Ramsey	arr.	11-15	12-20	5-20	8-20
	.. Douglas	arr.	12-25	1-00	6-00	9-00

ISLE OF MAN — GLASGOW.
1st July, to 2nd October, except where otherwise stated.
Daily unless otherwise stated.

			a.m. NS	p.m †	p.m. NS *	p.m. C †	.m. SO ‡
ISLE OF MAN	.. Douglas	dep.	8-15	1-15	4-15	5-00	4-15
	.. Ramsey	dep.	8-55	1-55	4-55	6-10	4-55
	..HALL CAINE AIRPORT	dep.	9-15	2-15	5-15	6-45	5-15
GLASGOW	..RENFREW AIRPORT	arr.	10-30	3-30	6-30	8-00	6-30
	.. Grosvenor Restaurant	arr.	11-00	4-00	7-00	8-30	7-00

NOTES.—NS—Sunday excepted.   C—Friday, Saturday, Sunday and Monday only.   † Service discontinues 1st September.
* Operates one hour earlier from 1st September.   SO‡—Sunday only from 5th September.
GROUND TRANSPORT PROVIDED BY COMPANY BUT SEATS MUST BE RESERVED FOR WHICH BOOKING FEE IS CHARGED: RAMSEY 3D. AND DOUGLAS 1/-

LINE 333.

GLASGOW — SKYE — NORTH UIST — SOUTH UIST — BARRA — GLASGOW.
1st July to 2nd October, except where otherwise stated.

						a.m. P	p.m. S ‖
GLASGOW	.. Grosvenor Restaurant	..	..	dep.		9-00	3-00
	..RENFREW AIRPORT ..	..	..	dep.		9-50	3-45
	..GLENBRITTLE AIRPORT	..	..	arr.		11-20	5-15
SKYE	..GLENBRITTLE AIRPORT	..	..	arr.		11-20	5-15
	..GLENBRITTLE AIRPORT	..	..	dep.		11-25	6-15
NORTH UIST	..SOLLAS AIRPORT	..	..	arr.		12-05 (p.m.)	..
	..SOLLAS AIRPORT ..	..	..	dep.		12-40	..
SOUTH UIST	..ASKERNISH AIRPORT	..	..	arr.		1-10	..
	..ASKERNISH AIRPORT	..	..	dep.		1-20	..
BARRA	..NORTHBAY ..	..	..	arr.		1-30	..
	..NORTHBAY ..	..	..	dep.		1-40	..
GLASGOW	..RENFREW AIRPORT ..	..	..	arr.		3-20	7-45
	.. Grosvenor Restaurant			arr.		4-00	8-30

GLASGOW — BARRA — SOUTH UIST — NORTH UIST — SKYE — GLASGOW.
1st July to 2nd October, except where otherwise stated.

						a.m. M	p.m. S ‖
GLASGOW	.. Grosvenor Restaurant	..	..	dep.		9-00	3-00
	..RENFREW AIRPORT ..	..	..	dep.		9-50	3-45
BARRA	..NORTHBAY	..	..	arr.		11-30	..
	..NORTHBAY	..	..	dep.		11-40	..
SOUTH UIST	..ASKERNISH AIRPORT	..	..	arr.		11-50	..
	..ASKERNISH AIRPORT	..	..	dep.		12-00 (p.m.)	..
NORTH UIST	..SOLLAS AIRPORT	..	..	arr.		12-30	..
	..SOLLAS AIRPORT ..	..	..	dep.		1-05	..
SKYE	..GLENBRITTLE AIRPORT	..	..	arr.		1-45	5-15
	..GLENBRITTLE AIRPORT	..	..	dep.		1-50	6-15
GLASGOW	..RENFREW AIRPORT ..	..	..	arr.		3-20	7-45
	.. Grosvenor Restaurant			arr.		4-00	8-30

Connections to Benbecula from North Uist or South Uist, and to Harris from North Uist, on demand.
NOTES.—M—Tuesday, Thursday and Saturday.   S—Saturdays only.   P—Monday, Wednesday and Friday.   ‖ July and August only.

married at Dumfries that July. Moving down south to Rochester, her airline career ended, though she continued to do a little flying. After Francis' death at Padstow, where they were then staying, she married Bill Orchard, a local fisherman, returning to Scotland after his death.

The summer of 1934 must have been rather depressing at Renfrew. A bold, visionary enterprise had been forced out of business by bigger battalions. They were now set to take over on a much smaller scale. Railway Air Services had made it clear that they didn't intend to take over Midland & Scottish Air Ferries Ltd.'s operations, nor did they, though they reintroduced the Glasgow to London trunk route, via Belfast, Liverpool and Birmingham. This should have been inaugurated on 20th August. However, bad weather disrupted the inaugural services, being flown by four-engined D.H.86 airliners — the full service went into operation on the 21st. This continued until after the Second World War and was run, as were other Railway Air Services' services for a particular railway, in this case, unsurprisingly, the LMS.

The Scottish Flying Club's progress, however, had been such that they were able to build a splendid clubhouse at Renfrew, designed by A.F. Wallace of

Noad & Wallace — it cost just under £6,000 and was opened in November. Little could they know of what it would become.

The 1st of December, also saw Sword's erstwhile associate, Edward Hillman, appear briefly on the London — Liverpool — Glasgow route in competition with Railway Air Services. On 30th April, that year, Renfrew had been granted full customs facilities, over a year later on 30th July, 1935, radio communcation came into use.

The withdrawal of Midland & Scottish Air Ferries Ltd. from the routes they had pioneered, opened them up to others unhindered by competing, commercial arrangements. Thus George Nicholson, from Newcastle, yet another bus operator, incorporated his Northern and Scottish Airways on 21st November, 1934, and began operations at Renfrew on 1st December, with a twice weekly Campbeltown and Islay service — charging thirty shillings to Campbeltown. Northern and Scottish Airways also took over the Scottish Air Ambulance service in January, 1935, and from 1st February, 1935, the Glasgow — Campbeltown service ran on weekdays, extending to Islay on alternate days. Later the service ran daily on weekdays, and on 17th May, a Renfrew to Isle of Man service with Dragons began, initially on three days per week; then daily; then six weeks after inauguration, twice daily. However, during May, 1935, financial control of Northern and Scottish Airways was taken over by Whitehall Securities, with Mr. J. de C. Ballardie replacing George Nicholson as Chairman, though the latter continued to serve Northern and Scottish Airways, and indeed it successors. Whitehall Securities built up a considerable interest in a number of the emerging UK airline companies, initially allowing them to trade under their own names. However, at the end of 1935, Whitehall merged their United Airways with Hillman's Airways and Spartan Air Lines, calling the new company Allied British Airways which soon became British Airways — the first British Airways! Northern and Scottish Airways had, by July, 1936, become a wholly owned subsidiary of Whitehall Securities/British Airways and had begun operating services outwith the West of Scotland for British Airways. They operated all British Airways Irish Sea services from 1st July, 1936, in addition to their original routes from Renfrew, which on that date, were integrated providing a circular Glasgow — Skye (Glenbrittle) — North Uist — South Uist — Glasgow service, with connections available to Barra, Benbecula and Harris as required. The inaugural flight to Skye (Glenbrittle) was flown in Dragon, G-ACFG, by David Barclay on 5th December, 1935. Northern and Scottish Airways Irish Sea routes were Liverpool — Belfast — Glasgow; Liverpool — Blackpool — Isle of Man — Glasgow; Belfast — Glasgow; Belfast — Isle of Man; Isle of Man — Carlisle. Quite a pattern, and on 7th August, 1936, the Air Ministry issued a licence allowing flying to take place from the beach at North Bay, Barra — a famous institution in Scottish civil aviation also still in use. A number of Spartan Cruiser aircraft were transferred to Northern and Scottish at the end of June, 1936, and served them and Scottish Airways until the outbreak of war. One aircraft, G-ACYK, crashed on the Hill of Stake, above Largs on January, 14th, 1938. Its remains were left there until July, 1973, when a Sea

King helicopter of Prestwick-based 819 Squadron Royal Navy, airlifted the remains to the Museum of Flight at East Fortune. In the curious phonetic alphabet of the times, its call sign was 'Scottish, Yokohama Kilogram', G-ADEL, being 'Eddystone, Liverpool'!

On 20th April 1936, with the 'Flying Flea' craze at it height, Houston Anderson was killed at Renfrew whilst flying one of them. Other crashes caused the aircraft to be grounded and many of these home-built aircraft were left abandoned all over the country.

Changes came to Northern and Scottish Airways in 1937. The Blackpool — Isle of Man — Belfast — Glasgow service was taken over by Railway Air Services in May, and on 1st June, Northern and Scottish Airways restarted direct Glasgow to Isle of Man.

With the formation of Scottish Airways in 1937, by combining Northern and Scottish Airways (renamed Northern Airlines for a short while) and Fresson's Highland Airways, together with parts of McBrayne's, (British Airways 50%, LMS Railway Co. 40%, David McBrayne 10%, with Scottish Airways and McBrayne's each owning 50% in Western Isles Airways — the holding co.), the basis for a co-ordinated transport system was created — a goal that has since eluded the transport industries of this country. Western Isles Airways Ltd., was formed in July/August, 1937. The re-organisation allowed greater, internal co-ordination of British Airways' internal services along with the those of Railway Air Services. This Scottish Airways, with its headquarters at Renfrew, was not related to the post-war Scottish Airlines, a subsidiary of Scottish Aviation Ltd. at Prestwick. The dominant position which the railway companies, particularly the LMS, had with travel agents, necessitated an accommodation with them and Scottish Airways, together with their parent. British Airways were, in fact, now working with Railway Air Services. The new Board had representatives of RAS on it. In the late 1930s, from about 1937, the UK airline scene divided itself into two — the Railway Group and the Whitehall Securities Group (British Airways and Scottish Airways).

Sensibly, Fresson continued to manage the northern operation from Inverness, opening a Renfrew — Perth — Inverness service on 3rd May, 1938, Nicholson was in charge at Renfrew, where the indomitable David Barclay remained as Chief Pilot. David Barclay, was born in Greenock, and educated at Greenock Academy. His family had a dairy business in the town. Scottish Airways' offices at Renfrew were in the building just on the right as you entered the airport. The newly instituted Air Transport Licensing Authority, in October 1938, granted Western Isles Airways the Glasgow — Islay and Glasgow — North Uist routes. Scottish Airways were granted, Inverness — Shetland and Kirkwall — Longhope — Westray — North Ronaldsay —Sanday — Stronsay.

Regulation of air transport was now being introduced in order to avoid wasteful competition, and provide a means of allocating Government subsidies. In the 1980s, after many attempts at this, deregulation became the order of the day. With war clouds looming in May, 1939, Scottish inaugurated services between Kirkwall and Glasgow. Like all other operators, all their services ceased on the outbreak of war on 3rd September, 1939.

Saro Cutty Sark of British Amphibious
Air Lines at Renfrew, 1932.

One of Railway Air Services' de
Havilland Rapides.

.H.86 G-ACVY 'Mercury' of Railway
ir Services at Renfrew, May 1939.

Imperial Airways D.H.86b airliner
G-ACPL 'Delphinus'. This was one of the
two which inaugurated Railway Air
Services Glasgow — London service on
20th, 21st August 1934.

Hillman's Airways Dragon at Romford bound for Paris — connecting service from Midland & Scottish Air Ferries' Glasgow run.

Eric Starling in white flying overalls with Aberdeen Airways' Short Scion at Renfrew on inaugural Aberdeen to Glasgow service, 10th September 1934. Eric Gandar Dower, second from left on the ground.

Small passenger (10 months old and a regular traveller) with father awaiting departure for the Hebrides.

Whilst the story of Midland & Scottish, Northern and Scottish, and then Scottish Airways, and their scheduled services, is central to the development of Renfrew from an airfield to an aerodrome, and finally an airport, the activities of Railway Air Services and 'The Manx Airway' with their trunk route 'The Royal Mail Route' between London and Birmingham, Liverpool, Belfast and Glasgow with connections to Manchester, Blackpool and the Isle of Man, provided an attractive pattern of internal air services from Glasgow's airport. Railway Air Services were granted the route licence by the ATLA for London — Glasgow, and Glasgow — Belfast in October, 1938, using D.H.86s, Rapides and sometimes aircraft from Imperial Airways.

Aircraft of many other companies and individuals used Renfrew's well worn turf. British Amphibious Airlines Ltd., formed in 1932, with two Saunders-Roe Cutty Sark amphibians were seen at Renfrew, Greenock and Rothesay Bay, along with British Flying Boats Ltd. who operated a service between Greenock and Belfast for a week in August, 1932, with their Saunders-Roe Cloud, *Cloud of Iona.*

Eric Gandar Dower, showman, aviator and MP's Aberdeen Airways began operating his Short Scion G-ACUV on an Aberdeen to Glasgow service in September, 1934. This aircraft was painted in a purple and yellow colour scheme!

Less well known, was West of Scotland Air Services formed early in 1935, and in addition to operating a service with Fox Moths between Greenock and Arran (Shiskine) with a single fare of twenty-five shillings, offered pleasure flights from Ettrick Bay, Bute. Another of Scotland's female pilots, Miss Margaret Cunnison flew for them, continuing until 1938, during which year a Short Scion Senior floatplane was used, with trips from Greenock to the Hebrides. They were also granted a five year contract with the Stornoway Trust to provide a Stornoway to Glasgow service. It was not operated, however, as it was feared they might violate the Sabbath!

The Empire Exhibition held at Bellahouston, Glasgow in the summer and early autumn of 1938, must have boosted Renfrew's traffic somewhat. North Eastern Airways, though based in London and operating up the East coast, flew a Newcastle — Glasgow service for the duration of exhibition and on its closure, one from Doncaster to Glasgow via Edinburgh. Airspeed Couriers and Envoys were used.

Other visitors included a few foreign aircraft, including the Junkers Ju 52/3m D-ANEN *Fritz Puetter* and a Messerschmitt Bf108.

During Scottish Airway's inaugural Renfrew — Perth — Inverness service on 3rd May, 1938, the redoubtable Major D.K. Michie, Provost of Renfrew, from 1930 to 1942 dropped his bombshell — Renfrew airport would be shortly closed. The Town Council's patience with the Air Ministry had become exhausted and unless the Ministry were prepared to designate Renfrew as a civil airport, the Council would shut it down. Provost Michie, factor to the Elderslie Estates was shrewd and astute, more than a match for the bureaucrats

Scottish Airways Spartan Cruiser
G-ACYK over Glasgow University, late
1930s being flown by Capt. David
Barclay. This was the aircraft which
crashed on the Hill of Stake near Largs on
14th January 1938. Its remains
eventually went to the Museum of Flight,
East Fortune.

April 1938 'shock announcement'.

and the Ministry, grudgingly conceded. The outbreak of war, however, overtook the short period initially covered by the designation and Renfrew was requisitioned and extended thus giving it a new lease of life.

The success of Clydeside shipbuilders and engineering concerns in aircraft production during World War 1 was not to be paralleled during the Second World War, though a number of Glasgow and West of Scotland firms contributed in different ways to aircraft production — Morris furniture for one.

The influential Clyde shipbuilder and industrialist, Sir James Lithgow, had attempted to ensure that Scotland would create an aircraft industry in the 1930s — it was losing on the automobile front and he proposed a multinational scheme involving American and Italian interests to produce, flying boats at the disused Caird shipyard in Greenock. As Charles Oakley recounts, the Air Ministry were characteristically unhelpful. Lithgow then formed a company, Scottish Aircraft Components, to assist firms to enter the aircraft industry. Little, however, was achieved.

It would seem that the Government regarded the Midlands as the Air Ministry's province and Clydeside, the Admiralty's — not too surprising perhaps, given the long standing relationships which must have been developed among all those engaged in shipbuilding at official and company levels.

That ubiquitous Devonian, Charles Oakley, who initially qualified as a Naval Architect at John Brown's and the University of Glasgow, was appointed the Air Ministry's Scottish Area Officer. During the period of the phoney war, he had been lecturing at the University. He had much to do with the development of the new Rolls-Royce Shadow factory at Hillington, and the Blackburn one at Dumbarton, where they built their infamous Botha torpedo-bomber. It is believed that a test report stated that — "this aircraft is difficult to enter, it should be made impossible!" They were also one of the firms which built the Short Sunderland flying boat, testing them at Rhu on the Gareloch. He was also involved with the establishment by Lockheed of their assembly and maintenance base at Renfrew. Among its many activities during the War, Scottish Aviation set up a flying boat servicing operation at Greenock, in fact using Caird's yard, and opening on 1st June, 1940. There was also a flying boat base at Largs. Among the unlikely sites for aircraft production was Scottish Aviation's use of an old warehouse at 39 West Campbell Street, in Glasgow City Centre. This was where SAL's first complete aircraft, Queen Bee, radio-controlled targets were built.

Charles Oakley's interests ran from industrial psychology to the film business, via Jean McGregor's Scotch Broth.

During the decade of the thirties, which saw the country go from deep economic depression to world war, Renfrew saw the departure of 602 (City of Glasgow) Squadron Auxiliary Air Force to Abbotsinch, the growth of the Scottish Flying Club into the leading organisation in its field, and the sustained development of commercial air transport.

Renfrew during the later 1930s.

German visitor, 1936? Messerschmitt BF 108.

G-ACSM, Spartan Cruiser II of Scottish Airways at Renfrew, May, 1939.

The thirties were the streamline age. Art, design and architecture adopted speed as a theme. The railway companies, particularly the LNER, who capitalised on it with their *Silver Jubilee* and *Coronation* trains in 1935 and 1937, and hauled by Gresley's superb streamlined A4 Pacifics, one of which *Mallard* captured the world's speed record for a steam locomotive of 126 m.p.h. in 1938. The LMS also entered the lists with the *Coronation Scot*. The seeds of an integrated transport system could have been sown then — or perhaps a monopoly? War, and its aftermath dramatically altered the scenarios.

Just after the outbreak of World War II, Scottish Airways, having been brought within the National Air Communications scheme, was among the first companies to resume services — Renfrew to Campbeltown and Islay, and thereafter others of the original routes were restarted. The evacuation of France saw Scottish Airways' unarmed Rapides pressed into service from 14th June 1940, returning north at the end of the month.

Though a few aircraft were lost, none to enemy action, Scottish Airways' war record is second to none — some commentators have stated that their operation was the most highly respected of all. They flew over 5 200 000 miles carrying over 71 500 passengers, more than all th other AAJC companies put together. They also carried 4 319 599 lbs of mail and 1 296 086 lbs of freight. In addition, of course, to maintaining the Air Ambulance service.

David Barclay, Jimmy Mitchell and many others had added a brave chapter to the history of Scottish flying.

During the war, Renfrew Airport was considerably developed and expanded, though not sufficiently to ensure its eventual survival. Its proximity to the Clyde and Glasgow's Docks in particular, King George V Dock — one of the few still surviving, made it ideal for the reception, assembly, repair and despatch of aircraft delivered by sea, or in the case of the Spitfires for Malta, the other way about. Abbotsinch, likewise, was handy for the Clyde with its tributary, the Cart, providing easy water born access. It was natural for Abbotsinch, therefore, to be transferred from the Royal Air Force to the Royal Navy. Walter Bell's reminiscences tell something of the wartime stories of the two places.

SCOTTISH AIRWAYS WARTIME TRAFFIC

	Passengers	Mail lb	Cargo lb	Miles flown
1940	9 832	584 595	120 226	583 563
1941	11 754	682 841	172 883	710 150
1942	11 495	833 157	197 540	804 579
1943	11 619	806 736	236 799	939 415
1944	12 395	799 510	241 909	979 803
1945	14 443	612 760	326 729	1 182 639
TOTAL	71 538	4 319 599	1 296 086	5 200 149

1939 figures cannot be broken to show Sept-Dec or 1945 figures from War's end to 31/12

R E N F R E W   A N D
A B B O T S I N C H
A T   W A R

A Memoir by W. A. M. Bell

WHEN an elderly grey-haired member of the Home Guard chased two small boys away from the fence at Renfrew Airport in 1941, he roused their curiosity and made it inevitable that they would return at the earliest opportunity. Activity at the airport on this early summer evening consisted of two D.H. Rapides, an Avro Anson and a Fairchild Argus which was preparing to take off. When the boys went back to the airport a few days later, the scene was much the same except that the Anson had gone and in its place was a Bristol Blenheim Mk.IV. The arrival of a Handley Page Harrow transport, at that time considered a large aircraft, convinced our two young friends that there was more to Renfrew than a couple of Rapides and a Blenheim, and it was then that they decided to make Renfrew a regular bicycle run. They soon realised that this was a very quiet airfield with only a few regular aircraft in the shape of D.H. Rapides, D.H. Dragons, D.H.86Bs and Blenheims. However, having seen a Harrow and being natural optimists, they persevered and soon their log books contained such types as the Airspeed Oxford, Miles Magister, Armstrong Whitworth Whitley Mk.III and Mk.V, the Bristol Blenheim Mk.I, the Hawker Hurricane and Supermarine Spitfire Mk.II. They did not know at the time that if their visits had started at the beginning of the war, their experiences would have been the same except for one burst of activity towards the end of 1940.

In November, 1940, No. 309 Squadron, flying Westland Lysanders, took up residence. They were to operate in exercises with many army units now based across the central belt of Scotland and these slow high wing aircraft soon became a common sight as they went about their business. The airport, mainly because of its position close to Glasgow, proved to be unsuitable, and the Squadron transferred to Dunino, Fife, in May, 1941.

The Rapides and Dragons were Scottish Airways machines and the D.H.86Bs that were more irregular in their appearances, belonged to Railway Air Services. They were all now under the control of the Associated Airways Joint Committee and were used to carry essential personnel and material to points around the country, but especially to the North and the Islands. These aircraft were painted in the standard brown and green camouflage colours with silver undersides. They had red, white and blue horizontal stripes under the registration, presumably to identify them as British to defending fighters. Windows were painted over to prevent passengers from seeing sensitive areas and installations. A small Air Transport Auxiliary unit, based at the airport, used the Fairchild Argus to pick up and deliver pilots who ferried aircraft from factories to Squadrons and Maintenance Units. The Blenheims, which arrived and departed with regularity had the clean, sharp look of the newly painted and were probably on delivery.

It was in May, 1942, that Renfrew Airport experienced its first large movement of aircraft when the Air Transport Auxiliary flew in fifty-four Spitfire VBs, fitted with tropical filters. They were destined for King George V Dock, where the United States aircraft carrier USS *Wasp* would load and transport them to within flying distance of Malta. On Sunday, 31st May, they presented an unforgettable sight as they were taken on Queen Mary transporters along Renfrew Road to the dockyard. It was the position of Renfrew in relation to the Clyde docks that made it the first choice for this ferry flight, and it was for this same reason that an even more momentous decision was taken which led to a total change in the importance of this small airport.

After the United States entered the war in 1941, it was decided to form two US Army Air Forces in Britain. These were to be the Eighth Air Force and the Ninth Air Force. The aircraft to equip these would have to be transported across the Atlantic and all the single-engined, and a large number of the twin-engined had been carried across by cargo vessel. The number of ships performing this task would now increase enormously, and they would require good, extensive port facilities. Such facilities existed in the Clyde and Renfrew Airport because of its position, was selected as the European terminal for aircraft brought over in this way. Major construction work was required and plans were drawn up to build three new hangars and two all-weather runways. By the end of the summer of 1942, all based aircraft had been transferred to RAF Abbotsinch and the airport closed. Most of the construction took place on a large area of uncultivated land to the north of Newmains Road. The short runway was completed within this area, laid out in the 03/21 direction and stretched from Renfrew Road in the north-west to Newmains Road in the south-east. It was 4020 feet in length. At the Renfrew Road end, a large gate was put in the fence to facilitate access for the partly constructed aircraft which were to be unloaded at King George V Dock, towed along the Old Renfrew Road, straight on to the 21 end of the runway and so up to the hangars. The hangars were built to the west of the short runway and bordered on the town of Renfrew. They were surrounded by extensive aprons for the storage of aircraft awaiting completion. The hangars were operated jointly by Lockheed Overseas and Airwork. The main runway stretched from the corner of the golf course and Hillington Road and lay in the 08/26 direction. It cut across Newmains Road and followed the line of the old grass landing area to end at the edge of Arkleston Road, giving it a total length of 6000 feet. By the middle of May, 1943, construction was almost complete, although there were large mounds of earth bordering the runways and Newmains Road was still open to the general public. Rapides and Blenheims were back operating out of the old hangars and it was left to the common sense of the local population to stop clear of the edge of the runway whenever an aircraft was landing or taking off. By the beginning of August, all work was completed and the airport was, once again, operating normally.

On 13th August, an American Cessna Bobcat was seen on the apron in front of the new hangars, which led to much speculation, but it was not until the beginning of September, that we began to get some idea of the roll of the new

Scottish Airways staff at Renfrew, 1944.

Scottish Airways, Southern Division Fleet, at Renfrew, 1944.

airfield. The first Republic P-47 Thunderbolts appeared on the flight line, and closer inspection disclosed a number at the back waiting to be worked on. After this with the P-47s, were Douglas Bostons for the RAF. These were not the first Bostons to arrive in the Clyde. Since 1942, Grumman Martlets and Bostons had been arriving at King George V Dock, where they had been unloaded on to lighters and towed by tug up the White Cart to an acceptance unit on RAF Abbotsinch, which had been operating for some time. The interesting thing about the Bostons that were brought in to Renfrew, was their desert camouflage of sand, mid-stone and sky blue. After completion at Renfrew, they faced a long ferry flight to the Middle East.

The summer of 1943 marked a large change in the two airfields in the Renfrew area. RAF Abbotsinch was transferred to the navy and became HMS *Sanderling* and remained as such until it closed in 1963, when work was started on the construction of Glasgow Airport. Thus Abbotsinch, as an airfield, disappeared. The image of Renfrew as a quiet, little airport also disappeared and in its place, we have the beginning of a bustling, active airfield. Early August saw the arrival of Supermarine Seafires, Hawker Sea Hurricanes, Fairey Swordfish and Grumman Martlets, which took up residence beside the Rapides and Blenheims at the old hangars. It was assumed that this was an extension of the naval aviation activity across the Cart. Before the end of September, the first North American P-51s and the photographic version, called the F-6, put in an appearance along with Lockhead P-38s — all destined for USAAF Squadrons in the south of England. The P-51 for the RAF, known as the Mustang, joined the Bostons and Martlets, and continued to arrive for the Fleet Air Arm. Very soon the visitors apron became a hive of activity, with Cessna UC-78 Bobcats, Douglas C-47s, Douglas A-20s, Boeing B-17s, and Consolidated B-24s, all making the circuit a very busy and interesting place. Multiplicity of new aircraft and the major modifications being made to those already in service, resulted in Renfrew being host to an increasing number of different types. On 30th December, there were twenty different types of aircraft on the airfield. Two of these were the civilianised Vickers Warwick painted similar to the local Rapides and an A-20G of the USAAF, known in the RAF as the Havoc. This aircraft, with its four heavy machine guns in the nose and its twin gun turret amidships, was a particularly aggressive looking machine.

By the beginning of 1944, activity at the airfield had reached such a high level that the arrival on the 21st of January, of sixteen Spitfires on a movement north, would have passed as part of the daily routine, except that it gained prominence when one of them misjudged the position of the ground and finished up a crumpled wreck. Fortunately the pilot managed to stagger off on shaky legs.

Among the many aircraft seen were some which could be described, at that time, as rare. These usually arrived singly, parked in front of the tower at the old hangars and departed the next day. Such a one was the Blackburn Roc which arrived on 29th January, 1944, and left the next day. It had been converted to a target tug and was painted in the appropriate colour scheme. The large gun turret, with which this aircraft had been fitted, was now missing, but it could still be distinguished from the Skua by its wing tips. Another that could be described as rare, was the Curtiss Mohawk, which turned up on 17th August. It remained beside the tower until the 19th, when it took off and no doubt went back to where it came from. It has been fairly widely reported that the Mohawks that were ordered for the RAF were sent directly to India and South Africa, and those that were not required were sold to Portugal. The handful to be found in this country were ex-French Air Force machines that had been flown here ahead of the German advance in 1940. Two models of the Bell P-63A Kingcobra were delivered to the R.A.E. at Farnborough for evaluation and one of them visited Renfrew on Monday, 18th September, 1944, leaving again on the 20th.

As well as aircraft which I have described as rare, we also had the arrival of the very latest types, some of which were not yet off the secret list. On the evening of Wednesday, 17th May, 1944, a Northrop P-61 Black Widow appeared from behind the hangars and taxied out to the 23 threshold for departure on a flight test. This was the first flight of the Black Widow from

Royal Navy Grumman Avenger, JZ 54l, as flown in by John Stroud at Renfrew, piloted by Airwork's 'Dutch' Holland, 1945.

Renfrew, but it was another month before it was acknowledged by the powers that be. This, despite the fact that a picture of a drawing of it in an American comic published in January, 1944, appeared in 'News In Pictures' of *The Aeroplane Spotter* of March, 9th. *The Aeroplane Spotter* was the most comprehensive and accurate periodical on sale to the general public during the war, and was usually first with news and pictures of the latest aircraft.

Another American fighter that arrived at Renfrew before it was officially released from the secret list was the Grumman F-7F Tigercat. Several of these large twin-engined single-seat fighters were towed up to the airfield from King George V Dock on Friday, 8th December, 1944. They appeared to be complete with no sign of plastic cocooning. The wings, outboard from the engines, were folded up over the fuselage, and they were painted medium blue with white undersides. Both the P-61 and the F-7F turned up in fair numbers, but never to anything like those of the P-51s and the P-47s.

The Fairey Firefly Mk.I, was a British naval fighter still on the secret list, that joined the Seafires and Hellcats at the south end of the airfield on Saturday, 2nd September, 1944.

It would not have been natural if we had not made every effort to seek out information and when this was not forthcoming, to jump to conclusions. One of our more sensible ones, was that the naval aircraft which appeared just after the re-opening of the airfield, were attached to a holding unit. This idea had to be changed when a dummy carrier deck was established at the 23 end of the main runway and the circuit started to fill with Seafires, Swordfish, Martlets and Vought Corsairs, all mixed up and all practising deck landings. A bit of spice was added to the scene when the batman had to keep waving them off, while a couple of Thunderbolts or a Lightning prepared to depart on a flight test. I did not ever see him bat in a Mustang, though he may well have done so. It soon became clear that the Martlets had been delivered first, through RAF Abbotsinch and then at Renfrew, had now been joined by Hellcats, Corsairs and Grumman Avengers. Like the F-7s, mentioned earlier, they always looked complete as if ready to be flown and were never seen at the airfield in a plastic cocooning nor with tails and propellers missing. The reason could be that they first went to Alexander Stephen & Sons at Linthouse. This was a well known shipyard on the Clyde and one of the buildings, or shops as they were called, was used for undertaking modifications to naval aircraft, and it is just possible that the aircraft mentioned were first taken there to be prepared before delivery to Renfrew for flight testing. It became increasingly obvious that the American aircraft arriving at the south hangars were recently off the production lines and that a lot of the flying taking place, included flight tests. We soon reached the conclusion that these aircraft must be part of the vast trans-atlantic ferry operation and that the formations of them, which were now leaving the airfield in ever-increasing numbers, were part of the onward delivery system.

Coinciding with all this activity was the almost daily arrival of two communication aircraft in general use with the navy. Both were very attractive machines and soon became firm favourites with local spotters. They were the Percival Q.6 Petrel, a twin-engine seven seater and the Beech UC-43 Traveller, which was a very sleek looking biplane that could carry up to five. We assumed that they were bringing in naval pilots to pick up aircraft for delivery.

Another new aspect of the aviation scene in the early months of 1944, was the increasing number of formations of aircraft that were appearing. Previously, where we would see single aircraft taking off and flying in, it now became more common to have small formations and groups. Deliveries were now always in groups of four and upwards. A typical note in the log book of this period reads, 'eight Avengers, six P-47s and a UC-45 Expeditor taxied out one after the other, and took off. All headed south. A little later, one of the Avengers came back.'

Of particular note, were the formations of C-47 Dakotas, which would arrive in groups of twenty or more. A little hindsight enables us to speculate on whether they consisted of sections of the large formations which were exercising with the airborne troops in the Spean Bridge area at this time. One such formation, consisting of twenty-eight aircraft, circled the airfield on the evening of 7th May, and landed in a stream. They refuelled and within a short time, were airborne and heading south again. Every day saw flights of five or six arriving to pick up equipment of some sort. These usually had Squadron codes which, although not widely known at the time, can now be accurately identified. For instance, the seven that arrived on 28th August, contained elements of the 88th Troop Carrier Squadron coded 'M2' and the 91st Troop Carrier Squadron coded 'L4'. After the invasion on 6th June, these formations were all too often ambulance flights. They would land on the main runway, taxi down the short and park angled out down at the Renfrew Road gate, where the ambulances would enter to pick up their loads.

As the weeks passed, activity at the airfield increased with more and more visitors arriving each day. Many of these seemed like old friends, their pictures having been printed in one or other of the numerous books and periodicals covering the war in the air. Most of these were from operational squadrons like the Douglas A-20G, '7G-G' of the 641st Bomber Squadron, or the North American B-25 Mitchell, 'EV-N' of 180 Squadron. This latter was operated by personnel of the Free Dutch Air Force. On an ever increasing number of days, aircraft arrived to find that they were unable to obtain parking space on any of the aprons and had to be directed to odd hardstandings off the perimeter tracks, normally used by heavy vehicles. One such was the B-l7F *Circe* of the 303 Bomber Group, which ended up next to Newmains Road providing a close up view for interested passers by.

Such intensive operations made it inevitable that there would, from time to time, be the occasional accident, and one of the most spectacular of these happened on 3rd October, 1944. By September, a large amount of wear and tear was showing at either end of the main runway, requiring immediate resurfacing. The airfield was considered too essential to close completely for any length of time, and so the work was planned to take place in sections. Approximately the first third, starting at the Hillington Road end, was taken out of service and the usual runway control car was positioned at the edge of the new threshold. October, 3rd, was a bright, sunny day with the circuit in constant use. In the early afternoon, a new shape taxied from behind the hangars and moved slowly round to the new threshold to take off on a flight test. This was a P-38 Lightning with an extended nose, which provided a compartment for a navigator. It was called a Droop Snoot Lightning and was an attempt to develop the Lightning into a bomber, flying in large formations and all dropping their bombs together from medium altitude. It was not a successful experiment

Flying was proceeding normally when the Droop Snoot returned from its test, and started a long grass cutter approach to the new threshold. The runway controller had come out of his car and was standing with a Very pistol at his side watching and waiting. What could have been only an involuntary twitch of the trigger finger, caused a red flare to shoot out, hit the ground and bounce high into the air. A very quick response on the throttle right on the point of touchdown led to three spectacular bounces and on the fourth touchdown, the nose-wheel broke off. The remainder of the landing was done with the nose ploughing a furrow up the centre of the runway. As was usual when something like this happened, the sky suddenly seemed to fill with aircraft. In no time, there were thirteen in the circuit, two of which were B-24s. They, along with several others, soon decided to seek a quieter areas of sky and moved across and landed at HMS *Sanderling*. Two of the others were A.A.J.C. Rapides, one of which landed on the short runway. The pilot of the other showed his expertise and the handling properties of this aircraft by landing on the perimeter track leading to the 23 end of the main runway. The pilot of the Lightning was fortunately able to walk away from it with only bad memories.

When Renfrew became the main terminal for fighters and light twin-engined aircraft from America, it began attracting examples of all such types, whether American or British. Moreover, this attraction was not confined to such aircraft, but included were many of the larger twin-engined machines and also examples of all the four-engined aircraft operating in the United Kingdom. In the summer of 1944, the airfield started to accept such aircraft to have actual work done on them. These were B-24 Liberators of the RAF, which flew in for modification by Airwork with a view to operations in the Far East and rumour had it that the modifications included provision for carrying essential personnel on the long ferry flight. Whatever was the reason, there was certainly considerable movement of RAF Liberators, of all types, in and out of the airfield in the following months. Their numbers continued to grow until there were as many as thirty lying waiting to be worked on.

The operational duties of most of the B-24s in the RAF could be determined by their colour scheme and most of these started to appear on the aprons. The commonest was the grey and white of Coastal Command, but there were also examples of the green, brown and black of the Atlantic Ferry Service and the all black of the Electronic Counter Measures Squadron. At this period in the war, we had only a vague idea of the actual operations of this last type and if we had heard of it at all, thought that it had something to do with morse keys and radio telephony. The Liberators continued to arrive until the end of 1945, by which time most of them were in natural metal finish. One of the most colourful was pale blue with white undersides, but what sort of operational role it previously performed, remained a mystery.

Another group of aircraft that turned up in the summer of 1944, were Vultee A-31 Vengeances attached to the RAF. These large dive-bombers were ordered from America in 1940, but were used in this role by the RAF only in the Far East. In this country, their functions were as target tugs and in dive-bombing training. It seemed unlikely that a Squadron operating in either of these roles would be established at an airfield as active as Renfrew and yet they remained on the airfield until February, 1945, and were seen to fly regularly. No information ever trickled through about their role and we finally assumed that they had been based at Renfrew in one of these categories, due to necessity. A similar mystery surrounded the group of Armstrong Whitworth Albemarles, which turned up on 28th April, 1945. It was presumed that these aircraft were attached to a Squadron, although they never were present in Squadron strength. They also flew regularly, but as they were generally used as glider tugs, or for carrying paratroops, their presence at Renfrew seems incomprehensible. The conclusion reached at the time, was that they had been converted to pure transports, similar to the Warwick, and that the Rapides and Warwicks were no longer capable of coping, thus requiring the Albemarles as additional carriers. Only once, as far as I know, did an Albemarle arrive at Renfrew towing a glider. This was an Airspeed Horsa, on 21st September, 1945, which, after landing, was transported to the back of the Art Galleries in Glasgow as one of a number of exhibits in an official show. By this time, the other Albemarles had left and only a mystery remained.

The pattern of activity at Renfrew was established in 1943, and continued through 1944 and 1945, the only difference being one of tempo and this increased steadily until the end of the war in Europe. Just as the build up in 1943 had been fairly rapid, so was the run down, when the requirement ended in 1945. At the end of June, 1945, there were still twenty-two different types of aircraft on the aprons, but by August, this number had been halved and from then, there was a gradual decrease. By the autumn, the aircraft permanently based at Renfrew were Fairey Baracudas, Supermarine Sea Otters, Grumman Hellcats and other naval types, along with more appearances from D.H. Mosquitos, Bristol Beaufighters, Avro Lancasters and Vickers Warwicks. Civil aircraft became more prominent and consisted mainly of Rapides, Avro XIXs, and Dakotas. There were other individual civil aircraft which arrived, probably the most interesting being the Trans-Canada Air Lines Avro Lancastrian. This aircraft visited Renfrew on several occasions in 1946, but that is another story.

*   *   *

My first visit to RAF Abbotsinch was in the spring of 1942, when the main aircraft operating from it were Bristol Beauforts, Handley Page Hampdens and Blackburn Bothas. The Beauforts and Hampdens belonged to the Torpedo Training Unit and the Bothas were newly built aircraft from the Blackburn factory at Dumbarton. These were flight-tested and held until required at an Operational Training Unit. The first day I visited Abbotsinch, the Beauforts and Hampdens were very active and a couple of Bothas took off and returned within the hour. A Lysander landed and a couple of Ansons could be seen tucked into the side of the hangars. These aircraft probably belonged to the Combined Operations Development Unit which was still based here at this time. Not a lot, but always very interesting.

Many visits followed, and numerous visitors added spice to each day's flying. A fair number of these visitors must actually have been from the Maintenance Yard, HMS *Sanderling*, like the Vought Sikorsky Chesapeake, which on 10th May, circled the field three times and landed. The existence of this unit was not known to us until several weeks later. It was based in the large hangars on the White Cart side of Abbotsinch Road with slipways leading down to the White Cart to facilitate the transfer of lease-lend aircraft from cargo vessels to the airfield. My experience during 1942 was that aircraft under charge of this unit were kept in these hangars, except when the numbers became so great that they were parked in the fields around them.

On a dull, wet day in June, 1942, I brought my bike to a sudden stop, because I had just realised that the fields on my left were full of aircraft, parked nose to tail. The lack of light and close packing allowed me to make out only Airacobras, Lightnings and Martlets. The Airacobras and Lightnings were so near the road that three steps would have put me within touching distance. The Lightnings, which were in American markings, moved on within a few days, but the Airacobras, which were RAF machines, stayed for several weeks and did a fair amount of local flying. The Martlets were always with us from then on, although not the same ones. This was the first time I saw any aircraft in those fields and it was their appearance that led me to realise that the buildings on this side of the road were also part of the airfield, and so to the discovery of this unit.

The airfield at that time started at the kink in Abbotsinch Road where a lane led up the north edge of the field to Yonderton Farm, and on to the main road, where turning to the right took you to the Red Smiddy and to the left, down past the present Loganair hangar to Paisley. The three hangars at this western end of the field housed the Beauforts and the Bothas. They were separated from the road by a small fence which gave something to lean against while examining the contents of the large aprons. No such fence existed alongside the lane, and for a period during 1942, piles of 250 lb. bombs were stacked about ten feet in from the edge of the lane, right up its length. They had no tails and were obviously unfused, they may even have been filled with concrete, but they made a handy seat from which to view the day's flying. Nobody bothered about you provided you kept away from the aircraft, which made life a bit easier during a period which was very distressing for most people.

As 1942 progressed, the tempo at Abbotsinch increased, not with more flying by the TTU, but rather from an increase in the numbers of aircraft turning up, which we now know were connected in some way to the Maintenance Yard. Bostons and Mustangs for the RAF became a common sight on the airfield and after testing they were ferried to operational stations. We soon realised that the arrival of an Anson was followed by the departure of several of these aircraft. Very often the visitors were aircraft we had never seen before, such as happened on the afternoon of 14th March, 1943, when a Lockheed Ventura, a Martin Maryland and a Percival Q.6 Petrel turned up. I had not seen any of these types before, although I was to see the Ventura and the Q.6 very often, later on in the war. The Maryland was never present in this country in any great numbers and I was to see the type again, on only two or three occasions.

The transfer of RAF Abbotsinch to the Navy meant that the Maintenance Yard now took over the whole airfield, which became known as HMS *Sanderling* and the only regular non-naval aircraft present were the Bothas. The number of aircraft on the field increased by leaps and bounds, partly caused by the arrival of Squadrons from aircraft carriers coming into the Clyde and partly by the to and fro movement of aircraft from Machrihanish and the naval stations on the East coast. At the beginning of May, 1943, I first recorded the arrival of the Curtiss Seamew, which was a development of the Kingfisher. The Seamew was never a success, being badly underpowered and somewhat unreliable. These aircraft were in an immaculate condition, which testified to their lack of flying hours. They lay out in the main airfield seemingly never moving and at one time, I counted forty-three. They remained for two or three months and then like all the others, disappeared.

The transfer of the airfield to the Navy acted to my advantage toward the end of 1943, when a Petty Officer, whose family were neighbours of ours, was posted in. Sunday was visiting day, and a friend and I took full advantage of this concession. One of the most memorable visits was on 13th August, 1944, when we inadvertently investigated the contents of a hangar, which was restricted to Officers and P.O.s only. There were two aircraft in the hangar, which attracted our attention. One was an all black Swordfish, with a large radome under the fuselage, between the undercarriage legs. This, I believe, was the main reason for the restricted entry to this hangar, as was explained in great detail later, it was a long-range version of the Swordfish and the large bulge was an extra fuel tank. It was as good a reason as any, but somewhat wasted as we already knew about radar domes and had examples of them on all sorts of aircraft. We also knew that there was nothing secret about extra fuel tanks. There was also in the hangar, a Barracuda in US navy colours and markings. It was more unusual than I realised at the time, as I have never been able to trace any reference or notes about it. This event is one that has stuck in my mind, and I can still see it as if it had happened only yesterday. HMS *Sanderling* at that time, contained examples of just about everything flying with the Fleet Air Arm, and it was only because we managed to gain entry to the airfield on numerous occasions, that we saw them. There were quite a number of station hacks, almost a unit in itself, containing such types as the Fairey Fulmar, the Gloster Sea Gladiator — which the Station Captain used as his personal aircraft — and the Swordfish, with twin cockpits instead of the large hole for the observer and gunner. There were Stinson Reliants, D.H. Tiger Moths, North American Harvards and even the odd Miles Master Mk.I. We moved heaven and earth to get a flight in the twin cockpit Swordfish, but to no avail. Everything else was present in all sorts of colour schemes and markings.

When Petty Officer H. returned to sea duty, we hurriedly searched around for another key to the door, and came up with an ATC uniform. This was used on countless occasions, both official and otherwise. The main advantage turned out to be contact with a young Sub. Lieutenant, who for some unknown reasons was condemned to look after cadets like us. For compensation, he was given a Tiger Moth, which he was only too anxious to use in the duty of providing air experience. A few of us acquired new air experience every week and needless to say, when not flying, we were poking our noses into everything in sight. Like most active airfields, as the war progressed through 1944, the number of aircraft increased with many complete Squadrons arriving for a rest — many needing extensive maintenance or a complete change of aircraft type. Every mark of Seafire turned up at some time or other, along with all sorts of Sea Hurricanes, in all sorts of colours. In 1945, there was an increase in types at the airfield which began to receive visits from Mosquitos, Beaufighters and other twin-engined types, although most of these landed at Renfrew.

On 19th June, Air Vice Marshal Tedder flew to HMS *Sanderling* in his personal Dakota on his way to receive the freedom of the City of Glasgow. This happened to be one of the days I was on the airfield, and I succeeded in gaining permission to see round this early executive styled machine. The body of the aircraft inside seemed much wider than usual, and it was fitted out as a sitting room, with large easy chairs and other forms of comfort. To someone still in the austerity following five years of war, it was like the last word in luxury.

The airfield was still fairly active in this first year after the end of the war, but gradually it became an enormous holding unit, where old wartime naval aircraft were dealt with before scrapping. There must have been well over five-hundred aircraft of all types lined up on the airfield in 1947. We always expected it to revert to the RAF as Abbotsinch, but this never happened, and so it remained as HMS *Sanderling* until it closed as a military airfield in 1963.

Royal Navy Grumman Hellcat at Renfrew, 1945. Liberators in background were being prepared by Lockheeds for service in the Far East.

Reminiscences from John Stroud

On Monday, 4th September, 1939, my wife and I sat upstairs in the club with Laura McDougal (Press Officer of Scottish Airways) as she was expecting to see hordes of German aeroplanes appear over the cemetery. By a hedge were the remains of Midland & Scottish's Avro Ten and Airspeed Ferry covered with branches to 'stop the Germans seeing them'.

I don't remember any whole aeroplanes there that day — it was a dead aerodrome.

1945

Airwork was rebuilding Grumman Avengers, most had broken firewalls after wheels-up landings. They were test flown by 'Dutch' Holland, an old airline pilot, then, when cleared as air-worthy, put on board a carrier in the docks, taken down the Clyde and lowered over the side. This met Lease-Lend requirements.

On 28th April, 1945, I went in FN901 but when taxi-ing out (fortunately not on take off) the starboard wing dropped, there were bangings and scrapings, and our starboard tyre complete with wheel rim was running away in front of us — corrosion!

On 27th December, 1945, I was lucky and got 15 minutes in Avenger II, JZ541. This was the last but one. We had to have parachutes but I don't think we were ever high enough to use them. We beat up the E-W runway at 230 mph!

Next day on Saturday, 29th, Holland flew the last one. He had been confined to low flights along the runway by Wishart, the air traffic controller, and he was lucky. As he passed the clubhouse, we saw black smoke trail back. David Prowse promptly downed Holland's drink, which he had left when told the Avenger was ready, and we rushed down to the tarmac — I think expecting to see a pall of smoke. But Holland got the wheels down and landed across the runways at Abbotsinch.

Liberators were being modified for the Far East by Lockheed. The code name SNAKE was on the rear fuselages. I think the war ended before any were finished.

P O S T - W A R
T H E   J E T   A G E

RAILWAY

AIR

SERVICES

SUMMER
TIME TABLE

RAS

APRIL 15th 1946 AND UNTIL FURTHER NOTICE

R.A.S.

THE cessation of hostilities in Europe on 8th May, 1945, saw Renfrew Airport mightily changed. Now, it covered more than twice its original area, and with proper runways — main 08/26 and subsidiary 03/21.

Both Scottish Airways and Railway Air Services had been making plans for the post-war development of their services, and together, they began again nearly a month before VE Day. On 9th April, 1945, Rapide G-AGLP opened the Renfrew — Prestwick — Liverpool — Croydon service — Prestwick being deleted from 8th May, and Renfrew, from which the aircraft positioned becoming the terminal. The route acted as a feeder for Trans-Canada Air Lines' service to Canada. In the summer of 1945, Scottish Airways inaugurated direct flights between Renfrew and Stornoway and were also operating Rapides on services from Renfrew to Campbeltown, Islay, Tiree, Benbecula, North Uist and Stornoway, together with Renfrew to Belfast, Railway Air Services served Belfast and Croydon via Liverpool, also with Rapides. Both Scottish and RAS were still operating within the AAJC organisation.

Renfrew itself, having been requisitioned by the Air Ministry for the duration of the War, was still owned by Renfrew Town Council, though in 1945, the Ministry offered to purchase the lands from the Council, asking them for a price. It took until 1948 for a valuation to be proposed. In the meanwhile, compensation was paid annually, equivalent to a rent — an arrangement which actually continued until 1960, when the Ministry submitted a draft Compulsory Purchase Order for the land. In the event, Renfrew Town Council granted the Ministry a 99 year lease, giving themselves the option of resuming control of the lands in the event of the airport being closed. Even as this was being minuted, on 2nd August, 1960, the public debate on a future airport for Glasgow had been re-opened. In all of this, Renfrew Town Council, with their wily Town Clerk, McCutcheon, had proved themselves worthy guardians of their ratepayers' interests.

The General Election of 1945, gave a landslide victory to the Labour Party, whose plans for the future of civil aviation were based upon nationalisation. Thus, the RAS proposals came to nought. They had fully expected to have them accepted, giving RAS and their associated companies, the dominant position on internal and European routes, *without subsidy* and with British equipment, when possible.

In the event, British European Airways Corporation, emerged from the European division of BOAC on 1st August, 1946, though between then and 1st February, 1947, Railway Air Services and Scottish Airways with other AAJC companies operated on British European Airways' behalf. Two Avro

XIXs were loaned to Railway Air Services by Avros during the autumn of 1945, one G-AGPG, was successfully used for a trial period by Scottish Airways on the Renfrew to Stornoway route. A number of these aircraft were ordered and delivered to Railway Air Services from November, 1945, and subsequently taken over by British European Airways. During May, 1946, 20-seat DC-3/C-47s began flying on the main routes of Railway Air Services including the services between Renfrew and London, and Renfrew and Belfast — the first Renfrew — London service being flown by G-AGZA on 20th May, 1946. They replaced the D.H.86s and, because of their larger capacity, the London/Glasgow fare was cut by £2.0s.0d. and, like the Avro XIXs, were actually operated by Scottish Airways.

The way Fresson and Nicholson were treated was shameful. Gandar Dower, as always the individualist, managed to retain his independence however, for a short while. At one point, it seemed that few of the existing senior staff would be retained, even David Barclay's future was in some doubt. In the event he became responsible for British European Airways' Air Ambulance unit based at Renfrew. A Scottish Division of British European Airways was instituted with George Nicholson at its head, and E.E. Fresson was given the job as Northern Area Manager — less than he had a right to expect. In the event, the arrangements didn't last long for the Divison was dissolved and George Nicholson dismissed in September, 1947. Fresson was made redundant at the end of March, 1948. As was to happen all too often in the future, political ideology and interference provided no basis for the successful conduct of an airline business or indeed, any business.

At Renfrew, British European Airways, took over on 1st February, 1947, using Junkers-Ju 52/3ms on certain Scottish routes, such as Renfrew to Belfast. Some of these had previously been operated for BEA by Railway Air Services and Scottish. They were wartime build machines, whose life expectations hadn't been long and with spares being difficult to obtain, they didn't last long — nice though they were to fly. One, G-AHOK, ran off the runway on to two ruts in the ground, which initially fitted the track of the wheels. Unfortunately, the ruts were not parallel and the aircraft was written off. On 19th December, 1946, DC-3/C-47 G-AGZA with a Scottish Airways crew, set out from Northolt, the then London terminal, for Glasgow. Due to icing problems, the aircraft wouldn't climb, and ended up perched on a suburban roof at 46, Angus Drive, Ruislip. Fortunately none of the four crew nor the single staff passenger was hurt, though the householders must have been rather surprised! Capt. W.J. Johnson, forever after known as 'Rooftops Johnson', and Ian Crosbie, the second officer, went on to serve with British European Airways. The house was afterwards given the name it still possesses — 'Dakota's Rest'. British European Airways' first service from Northolt to Renfrew was flown by DC3/C-47 G-AGYZ under the command of Capt. John Ramsden, arriving in Glasgow at 4.00 p.m. That evening, a party was held in the Central Hotel, Glasgow, to mark the passing of what might be called, the pioneering chapter, in Scottish air transport.

Renfrew's 'terminal' was converted out of the Scottish Flying Club's

RENFREW

Date	Type		Operator	Reg.
21.8.50	VICKERS VIKING IA		HUNTING AIR TRAVEL	G-AHPI
	FAIREY FIREFLY 5 (handed over)		R.N.	WB233 (277)
	DOUGLAS DC-3 DAKOTA		B.E.A	G-AJIA
	D.H. 89 RAPIDE		B.E.A	G-AGSH
	AIRSPEED CONSUL		AIR ENTERPRISES	G-AJNE
	D.H. 89 RAPIDE		B.E.A	G-AGSK
	SUPERMARINE SPITFIRE 22 (LO:A)		R.A.F	PK518
	SUPERMARINE SPITFIRE 22 (LO:B)		R.A.F	PK369
	SUPERMARINE SPITFIRE 22 (LO:D)		R.A.F	PK349
	SUPERMARINE SPITFIRE 22 (LO:E)		R.A.F	PK621
	SUPERMARINE SPITFIRE 22 (LO:F)		R.A.F	PK395
	SUPERMARINE SPITFIRE 22 (LO:G)		R.A.F	LA319
	SUPERMARINE SPITFIRE 22 (LO:J)		R.A.F	PK547
	SUPERMARINE SPITFIRE 22 (LO:K)		R.A.F	LA315
	SUPERMARINE SPITFIRE 22 (LO:L)		R.A.F	PK321
	SUPERMARINE SPITFIRE 22 (LO:M)		R.A.F	LA267
	SUPERMARINE SPITFIRE 22 (LO:N)		R.A.F	PK651
	SUPERMARINE SPITFIRE 22 (LO:O)		R.A.F	LA227
	SUPERMARINE SPITFIRE 22 (for Middleburgh STF)		R.A.F	PK325
	N.A. HARVARD II (AAI:X)		R.A.F	KF584
	N.A. HARVARD II (LO:Y)		R.A.F	KF374
	N.A. HARVARD II (AAI:2)		R.A.F	KF389

RENFREW

Date	Type		Operator	Reg.
17th Nov'51	DOUGLAS DC-3 (Pionair)		B.E.A.C.	G-AMFV
	DOUGLAS DC-3 (Pionair)		B.E.A.C.	G-AJHY
	DOUGLAS DC-3		B.E.A.C.	G-AHCU
	DOUGLAS DC-3 (Pionair)		B.E.A.C.	G-ALXM
	DOUGLAS DC-3 (Pionair)		B.E.A.C.	G-AMJX
	DOUGLAS DC-3 "ST. COLMILLE"		AER LINGUS	EI-ACE
	D.H. 89 RAPIDE		B.E.A.C.	G-AHKT
	D.H. 89 RAPIDE		B.E.A.C.	G-AHKV
	D.H. 89 RAPIDE		B.E.A.C.	G-AGSH
	D.H. 89 RAPIDE (New Colour)		B.E.A.C.	G-AGPH
	D.H. 89 RAPIDE (New Colour)		B.E.A.C.	G-AGUR
	D.H. 89 RAPIDE		B.E.A.C.	G-AGSK
	D.H. 89 RAPIDE		B.E.A.C.	G-AJSK
	D.H. 89 RAPIDE (Burned)		B.E.A.C.	G-AH??
	D.H. 89 RAPIDE		AIR ENTERPRISES	G-AKRS
	D.H. 89 RAPIDE		AIR ENTERPRISES	G-AKOB
	D.H. 89 RAPIDE		AIR ENTERPRISES	G-ALWY
	AIRSPEED CONSUL		AIR ENTERPRISES	G-AIOT
	AIRSPEED CONSUL		AIR ENTERPRISES	G-AIOV
	PERCIVAL PROCTOR		AIR ENTERPRISES	G-AIHG
	GLOSTER METEOR 7 (LO:W)		R.A.F	WF773
	D.H. 100 VAMPIRE 5 (LO:C)		R.A.F.	WA182

Type		Operator	Reg.
DOUGLAS DC-3 (Pionair)		B.E.A.C.	G-AJZC
DOUGLAS DC-3 (Pionair)		B.E.A.C.	G-AHZZ
7 UNCOLOURED AIRCRAFT IN OPEN			
CANADAIR F.86E		R.C.A.F.	19194
" " (NO.410 Sqd)		" "	19181
" "		"	19173
"			19184
"			19182
"			19185
"			19186
3 UNCOLOURED AIRCRAFT IN HANGAR			
CANADAIR F.86E		R.C.A.F.	19183
" "		"	19189
" " [410 Sq. AH.]		"	19178
4 COLOURED AIRCRAFT BESIDE HANGAR			
CANADAIR F.86E (Nose Sqd)		R.C.A.F	19179
" " 410 Sq		"	19171
" "		"	19135
" " 410 Sq. AH.		"	19176

Aircraft	Operator	Registration
N.A. Harvard II (DMK·F)	R.A.	FT361
Douglas DC-3 Dakota	B.E.A	G-AHCC
Douglas DC-3 Dakota	B.E.A	G-AJIB
Douglas DC-3 Dakota	N.W.A	G-AGMF
D.H.89 Rapide	Air Enterprises	G-AKRS
D.H.87 Hornet Moth	C.B. Mills	G-ADKK
Airspeed Consul	Air Enterprises	G-AIOT
Airspeed Consul	Air Enterprises	G-AIOV
Percival Proctor I	Air Enterprises	G-AIHG
Douglas DC-3 Dakota "St..."	Aer Lingus	G-ACLM
Douglas DC-3 Dakota	B.E.A	G-AHKK
D.H.89 Rapide	B.E.A	G-AHGH
Douglas DC-3 Dakota	B.E.A	G-AHCV
Avro Anson 21 (hene R-CR2)	R.A.F	VV269
D.H.89 Rapide	B.E.A	G-AHSK
Douglas DC-3 Dakota	B.E.A	G-AHCB
Douglas DC-3 Dakota "St Declan"	Aer Lingus	G-AHCL
Douglas DC-3 Dakota	B.E.A	G-...
Fairey Firefly I (landed wheel)	R.N.	MB728

Aircraft	Operator	Registration
S. Spitfire 22 (Lo·L)	R.A.F	PK32.
Vickers Viking (New Colours)	B.E.A.C.	G-AMG
Airspeed Oxford	R.A.F	HM739
Gloster Meteor 7 (Lo·V)	R.A.F	WF846
D.H.100 Vampire 5 (Lo·G)	R.A.F	WA427
D.H.100 Vampire 5 (Lo·L)	R.A.F	WA315
N.A. Harvard 2 (Lo·Z)	R.A.F	KF920
N.A. Harvard 2 (A V...)	R.A.F	KF699
Douglas Skyraider (CW·)	Royal Navy	WT945
Douglas Skyraider (CW·)	Royal Navy	WT946
Douglas Skyraider (CW·)	Royal Navy	WT947
Blackburn Firebrand 5A	Royal Navy	EK614
N.A. Harvard	Royal Navy	EZ374
Fairey Firefly I (MF...)	Royal Navy	PP423
Fairey Firefly 5	Royal Navy	?
Fairey Firefly 5	Royal Navy	?
Fairey Firefly 6	Royal Navy	WJ111
Douglas DC-3	B.E.A.C.	G-AGIP
Douglas DC-3	B.E.A.C.	G-AGZ1

Park containing 22 aircraft in cocoons

Aircraft	Operator	Registration
Canadair F86E (No.410 Sqn)	R.C.A.F	19122
" 441 Sqn BT·	"	19134
" 461 Sqn BT·	"	19142
" 410 Sqn AMT	"	19144
" "	"	19147
" "	"	19150
" "	"	19152
" "	"	19153
" "	"	19154
" "	"	19155
" "	"	19156
" "	"	19157
" "	"	19158
" "	"	19160
" "	"	19161
" "	"	19162
" "	"	19165
" "	"	19166
" 410 Sqn AM·	"	19170
" "	"	19172
" "	"	19175
" (No.410 Sqn)	"	19177

distinctive '30s style Clubhouse of 1934, and the adjacent hangar. Access being gained by cracking open the hangar doors! Gates 1, 2 and 3 provided rudimentary viewing areas.

British European Airways introduced a London — Copenhagen — Glasgow service on 12th August, 1947, using the new Vickers Vikings — the first service being flown by Capt. 'Bill' Baillie, another former Scottish Airways' pilot, in G-AIVC *Vernon*. Sadly, the service failed to live up to expectations and ceased that December.

Political interference in British European Airways' affairs led to the resigation of Gerard d' Erlanger and J.V. Wood, early in 1949, and their replacement by Lord Douglas of Kirtleside and Peter Masefield. Sholto Douglas had had a most distinquished career in both the RFC and RAF, retiring as a Marshal of the Royal Air Force. Peter Masefield had already begun making his long and varied career in British civil aviation — they were to make a powerful team. Robert McKean became British European Airways' Manager for Scotland, based at Renfrew, and he too would serve his company and Scotland, with distinction.

On 28th September, 1947, the shape of things to come was seen at Glasgow's Hampden Park, in the shape of two of British European Airways experimental helicopter unit's Sikorsky S-51s. In fact one was owned by Westlands and flown by Alan Bristow. He would go on to form a very successful helicopter company of his own. Who would have thought then of the role helicopters would play, twenty or so years later, in the development of the oil and gas resources of the North Sea. Also in 1947, British European Airways introduced a number of new air mail services from Renfrew to the Western Isles.

The Scottish Flying Club had been given official notice to quit Renfrew in May, 1947, and it was an understandably sore point with them that no compensation was payable to them with respect to their buildings, now in use as Renfrew's terminal. It was scant reward for their magnificent efforts pre-war.

Early in 1948, British European Airways rationalised their aircraft maintenance facilities, transferring DC-3 overhauls to a new base at Renfrew from Liverpool, utilising the wartime Lockheed hangars. The Scottish Rapides, and subsequently the Herons, were also maintained there. In July 1949 due to the state of Abbotsinch, 602 returned to their birthplace at Renfrew, though aircraft would still be ferried to Abbotsinch for maintenance. Transiting through were the Spitfire 24s of the RAF's No.80 Squadron, who flew their aircraft to Renfrew, and then left for the Far East by carrier from King George V Dock.

1950, saw British European Airways inaugurate a Renfrew — Manchester — Paris service during April. However, lst August, brought the prototype Vickers Viscount 630, G-AHRF, to the airport, whilst on a month's commercial flying. At long last, in January 1951, Glasgow's fighter squadron, 602, was re-equipped with Vampire jets, and little whistling twin-boom aircraft became a familiar sight over Clydeside, along with the two Meteor 7 trainers. The deteriorating

Scottish Airways personalities in 1946 in front of their offices at Renfrew.
L. to R. — Bill Cumming, Capt. David Barclay, George Nicholson, Bill Mann.

G-AGZA, of Railway Air Services on the first DC-3 service, 20th May, 1946.

One of Railway Air Services' Avro XIXs at Renfrew, early in 1946.

DC-3, G-AGYZ, in Railway Air Services' colours, plus BEA 'speed-key' on fin, Renfrew, 1946.

A BEA's Junkers Ju 52/3m, 1947.

BEA Dragon Rapide at Renfrew, 1950, in original livery.

Air Enterprises at Renfrew 1950/51.

BEA Dragon Rapide in new livery.

BEA de Havilland Heron 1B, G-AOFY, 'Sir Charles Bell' at Renfrew. This was the aircraft which crashed on Islay, whilst on an air ambulance mission.

Air ambulance stalwart, BEA Heron, G-ANXA, at the Paisley end of Renfrew's runway 08/26.

BEA 'Dakota' freighter landing at Renfrew in the early fifties — note original BEA colour scheme.

Two of BEA's newly converted 'Pionair', class DC-3s at Renfrew, c.1951/2. Note different livery styles.

Pionair, G-ALXN, 'Sir Henry Royce' was for a time, one of the two Rolls-Royce Dart powered Dakotas.

BEA 'Dart' Dakota, G-ALXN 'Sir Henry Royce', used with its sister aircraft, G-AMDB 'Claude Johnson', on freight work to gain experience with turbo-props prior to Viscount's entry into service.

G-ALTT 'Charles Grey' flew BEA's last DC-3/Pionair service flight to Renfrew, April, 1962.

BEA Maintenance Base, Renfrew ('Lockheed Hangars').

Arrival of first propellor-turbine aircraft at Renfrew, prototype Vickers V.630 Viscount, G-AHRF, 1st August, 1950.

One of BEA's then, new Vickers Vikings, G-AHPR, 'Verity'.

BEA Viking, now converted to 'Admiral Class', G-AJJN, 'Sir Charles Napier' at Renfrew in the 1950s.

Viscounts V.70l, G-AMOB, 'William Baffin' and V.806, G-AOYN, 'Sir Isaac Newton' at Renfrew, 8th May, 1961.

BEA's new colour scheme of 1960 displayed by Viscount V.802, G-AOJB, 'Stephen Burrough'.

Vickers V.951 Vanguard G-APEB 'Bellerophon' at Renfrew, May 1961.

The new terminal as seen from a Vanguard.

BEA Argosy freighter and Handley Page Herald, G-APWB, April, 1962.

G-APRM, one of BEA's Armstrong Whitworth Argosy 102 freighters, 1st

June, 1962. They were replaced by 222s, including G-ASXP, seen taxying in on 25th June, 1965.

Shape of things to come — a Bell 47, G-AKFB, one of BEA's original helicopters at Renfrew on 2nd July, 1963.

Spitfire 21, LA269, (later coded RAI-H then LO-H), at Renfrew, Saturday, 2nd July, 1949. 602 Squadron had just moved over from Abbotsinch.

This Spitfire 22 PK321 was the last of 602's to leave Renfrew, in December 1951.

Puzzle picture — two Spitfire 22 or 24s at Renfrew, 2nd July, 1949. Could they be from the batch on their way to Far East for 80 Squadron?

Line-up of 602 Squadron Spitfire 21s and 22s at their Renfrew dispersal, 1949.

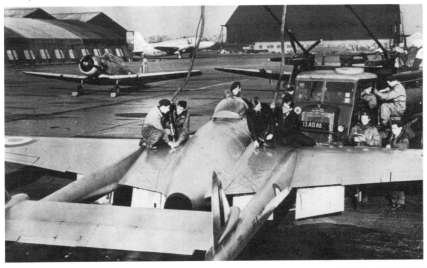

602 Squadron's new de Havilland Vampire jets on show to the press, Saturday, 27th January, 1951, at Renfrew.

The Royal Navy at Renfrew. Blackburn Firebrand, EK664, 1950/51.

An elegant de Havilland Sea Hornet takes-off on test-flight from Renfrew, c. 1951.

RAF visitor — 43 Squadron, Gloster Meteor T.7, VW488, at Renfrew, February, 1951.

One of 602's Vampire FB.5s.

602 Squadron also had Meteor T.7s, one of the first WF773, LO-W, lands at Renfrew.

RAF Pembroke C.I., WV703, 1st July, 1963.

RAF, V.I.P. de Havilland Devon, VP968, 8th July, 1964.

Avro Shackleton MR.3, XF709, 'D', of 120 Squadron, from RAF Kinloss, landing at Renfrew on 12th August, 1964.

Military version of the Vickers Viking was the Valetta. WD157, visits Renfrew on 7th April, 1965.

Avro Andover CC.2 of the Queen's Flight, 8th April, 1965.

One of the RAF's 'faithful Annies', Avro Anson TX229, 27th May, 1964.

Royal Navy Percival Sea Prince from RNAS Brawdy, WF138.

Thunderjets at Renfrew on delivery to Europe, Summer, 1951?

USAF, North American Mustangs at Renfrew — being prepared for shipping back to USA from the Clyde, 1953.

On delivery to Europe, Beech L-23A Twin Bonanzas, for the US Army, with Republic F-84E Thunderjets for the USAF, 1953.

U.S. Army de Havilland Canada Otter, 1st July, 1965.

U.S. Navy, North American SNJ-5, better known as the Harvard from the carrier, USS Franklin D. Roosevelt, anchored in the Clyde, 1954.

French Air Force Nord Noratlas at Renfrew, 21st June, 1965.

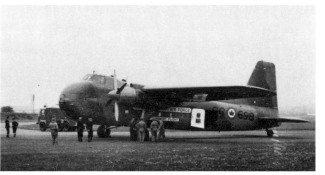

United States Navy Convair R4Y-1 141021, 14th April, 1965.

RCAF Bristol 170 Freighter, after emergency landing, 1960.

One of the first delivery of RCAF Sabres landing after a test-flight at Renfrew, Nov/Dec. 1951.

international situation caused the call-up of the auxiliaries in the Spring of 1951, and 602 went to Leuchars for three month's intensive training, alongside the regular resident, 43 and 222 Squadrons. On their return in July, they found their dispersal area and Bessoneau hangars occupied by the United States Air Force, whose cocooned Republic F-84 Thunderjets had been delivered by the time honoured method to King George V Dock, and were now being prepared for delivery to Europe — a squadron of Lockheed USAF F-80 Shooting Stars had preceeded them in 1948. The author, on one of his spotting visits recalls, seeing the F-84s from the vantage point of the adjacent playing fields and having to ask a friendly American what they were!

More surprises were in store, for in November, the swept-wing North American Sabres of No.410 Squadron, Royal Canadian Air Force, arrived at King George V Dock on board the carrier HMCS *Magnificent*. The aircraft were decocooned at Renfrew and flown to North Luffenham. Along with them, were the first early warning Douglas AD-4W Skyraiders for the Royal Navy. 602's new Vampires and Meteors looked just a little old-fashioned alongside the supersonic Sabres. At the same time, with Abbotsinch having its runways rebuilt and the Navy's RNVR 1830 Squadron 1830 having moved to Donibristle, Renfrew, was being used to service a host of naval aircraft — Fireflies, Firebrands, Sea Furies and Sea Hornets, among them. The early fifties at Renfrew were not without variety to the spotter. Ansons from Turnhouse came over regularly to give ATC cadets some air experience — parachutes being donned by the lads in the hangar.

Foreign visitors then were few, if the daily Aer Lingus flights from Dublin are discounted. Aer Lingus, had been given the monopoly of services to and from Dublin, using DC-3s and, for a while, Bristol 170 Wayfarers. In 1958, they introduced the elegant Fokker Friendship to airline service — between Dublin and Glasgow with Viscounts following later, and for a short time, Carvairs.

British European Airways, meanwhile, had had their large fleet of DC-3s converted into 32-seat 'Pionairs' by Scottish Aviation, complete with new radios and 'air stairs'. A few, called 'Pionair Leopards' could be quickly changed into freighters. Their new names recalled the great pioneers of British aviation. Vikings became the mainstay on the London route until the Viscount was introduced, initially, on the new 'Clansman' service in October, 1953, eventually, taking over that route entirely. Pionairs took over all the Scottish services except that to Barra and the Air Ambulance in October,1952. The first service was by G-ALXL *Charles Rolls*, Capt. Yorston to Tiree. A few Rapides soldiered on until two four-engined de Havilland Herons were delivered in 1955.

In 1953, despite the post-war stranglehold which the state imposed upon air transport, Hunting, later Hunting-Clan, Air Transport, under an associate agreement with British European Airways, ran services between Renfrew, Newcastle and London, and after much delay, 602 Squadron moved back to Abbotsinch during April, 1954. That year saw Renfrew's new terminal opened by the Minister of Transport and Civil Aviation on 26th November. It was a striking example of contemporary architecture designed by William

Renfrew, post-war. Note, Dragon Rapide, DC-3 and Ju 52, c.1947.

Viscounts of B.E.A., G-ANHE, G-AMOP, Renfrew.

Inside Renfrew's new terminal, 1954.

Renfrew's new terminal, 1954. The City
terminal was at St Enoch's Square.
Regular coach services ran to the Airport.

From the new control tower.

The old hangars and the Scottish Flying Club's Clubhouse, formerly Renfrew's terminal, now in use by Scottish Aviation Ltd. for the overhaul of RCAF and West German Air Force Sabres, and RCAF CFl00s, T-33s, 1957.

Scottish Aviation Ltd. using one of the former Lockheed hangars for maintenance of Royal Canadian Air Force aircraft.

German Air Force Sabre on test at Renfrew, late 1950s.

RCAF, Avro Canada CF-100, awaiting overhaul at Renfrew, late 1950s.

Aer Lingus DC-3 from Dublin, landing over the road at Arkleston.

U.S. Air force Lockheed F-80 Shooting Stars at Renfrew, 13th August, 1948 — on their way to Europe via the Clyde.

EI-AFS, 'St. Senan' one of Aer Lingus' Bristol 170 Wayfarers at Renfrew, summer 1953.

Aer Lingus was the first airline to put the Fokker F.27 Friendship into service. Here, EI-AKD, 'Flannan' is seen at Renfrew on the Dublin run.

One of Aer Lingus' Vickers Viscounts, EI-AMA, 'St. Conieth' lands at Renfrew with Braehead power station in the background.

The Aviation Traders Carvair was a conversion of the DC-4 for car carrying. Aer Lingus', EI-AMR, 'Iarflaith' touches down at Renfrew on 16th May, 1964.

School trip to Norway by Renfrewshire pupils, summer, 1957. The author's wife is third from left.

Kinninmonth. Sadly, after Renfrew's closure, despite some efforts, it wasn't possible to find it a new use and secure a future for the building. The old hangars of 1917/18 and Scottish Flying Club 'terminal' of 1934 were then used by Scottish Aviation Ltd. for the overhaul of Royal Canadian Air Force Sabres, Lockheed T-33s and Avro Canada CF-100s. Renfrew's runway limitations caused problems, particularly to the CF-100s, and the work was transferred to Prestwick in 1959/60.

A small charter company, Air Enterprises, had established a base at Renfrew in 1949, with Rapides and Airspeed Consuls, with which they performed ad-hoc charters, and Army co-operation work. They also had a single Percival Proctor based at Renfrew, but ceased operations in 1953.

During the fifties, the two Icelandic airlines began operating from Renfrew with Flugfelag Islands/Icelandair's famous Douglas DC-4 *Gullfaxi*, a regular visitor. Viscounts were introduced in 1957 on the Reykjavik — Renfrew — Copenhagen route. However, a transatlantic service was provided by Loftleidir, though it wasn't exactly direct — a stop in Iceland being required by the DC-4 and subsequently DC-6Bs — further international services were provided by Sabena to Brussels, and Ostend. Around this time, the debate about a future airport for Glasgow broke out in earnest. Proposals had been made a few years earlier for a limited expansion of the airport, however, it was realised that Renfrew's restricted site and location could never cope with the new, large jet transports then in prospect. Even the Vanguards which replaced the Viscounts on British European Airways' London route, were, at times, on the margins of operational suitability. The Renfrew/Prestwick/Abbotsinch/central airport arguments reflect little credit on the participants and it should be noted that after the Ministry of Aviation announcement in November, 1960, that Abbotsinch had been chosen to replace Renfrew, Glasgow Corporation indicated that they were far from enthusiastic about taking on the potential, financial responsibilities which would fall upon them and their ratepayers. A favourable financial deal soon sorted that out and the rest is history. During the 1950s, air transport had developed and expanded greatly. The jet-age was really inaugurated in air transport during 1958, after the disappointment of the Comet in 1954. Over the fifteen years from 1950 to 1965, passenger traffic at Renfrew grew from 131 789 to 1 276 623 per annum.

Renfrew's final six years witnessed a kaleidoscope of aeronautical activity. Handley Page Dart Heralds began flying on British European Airways' Scottish routes and Armstrong Whitworth Argosy freighters made their appearance. Few, however, will forget the nightly drone of Dan-Air's, Avro Yorks on freight charter for British European Airways, or Derby Aviation's Miles Marathons and Canadair Argonauts in the late 1950s and 1960s.

Would many have thought that Euravia whose Lockheed Constellations began operating in 1960, would grow into Britannia Airways, one of the UK's major operators, with a considerable presence at Glasgow Airport, thirty years later? Likewise, Capt. Duncan McIntosh's Capital Services (Aero) Ltd. which established itself at Renfrew, with a single Piper Apache, G-ARBN, in 1961, grew into Loganair on 1st February, 1962, and later

Women's Junior Air Corps, at Renfrew. Their Fairchild Argus, G-AIYO, 'Grey Dove' on right.

1815-2015
4 - July 1962 Renfrew
G-APEC, PEG, PEO Vanguards BEA
G-AOYJ, PJU, PIM, Viscount 806 BEA
G-AMOC, NHA, MOT, Viscount 701 BEA
G-AMOD Viscount 701 BEA
G-APWB Dart herald 102 Bea overhaul in Hangar
G-APWC, GAPWD Dart herald Bea
G-APRM argosy 102 BEA
G-ANXA GANXB Heron 1b Bea
EI-AKG EI-AKC F27 Aer Lingus
TF-ISU Viscount 759 Icelandair
G-AMSN DC3 Starways
G-ANTD DC3 Derby AW
G-AKNB DC3 Silver city
G-ARHL Aztec 250 Mcvitie & Price Ltd
G-APZF Apache 160 Ancock and Priestley
G-ARMH Aztec 250 } Duncan Logan
G-ARHV Tripacer 160 } (contractors) Lt.
G-ARFF Queen Air Dav J Ashmore.

became 'Scotland's Airline', and a member of the Airlines of Britain Group.

The Glasgow Flying Club emerged from Loganair, during 1963, and a rather different 'Loganair' was the great Scottish entertainer Jimmy Logan who flew from Renfrew in his Miles Gemini G-AJWC. He had learnt to fly at Perth with the much loved Tom Blyth — an instructor in the mould of the Scottish Flying Club's, John Houston, and like him, being tragically killed in a flying accident.

The end of an era came on 19th May, 1962, with the 11.35 a.m. arrival at Renfrew of DC-3 'Pionair'/Leopard, G-ALTT *Charles Grey*, from Islay and Campbeltown on the last flight by one of these superb aircraft in British European Airways' service. An appropriately named aircraft as C.G. Grey had written of Renfrew in the Aeroplane. However, another era had begun with Renfrew handling its first pure-jet transport — EC-ARI *Isaac de Albeniz* a Sud-Aviation Caravelle VIR on 28th April that year, and Cambrian Airways inaugurated their Glasgow — Manchester — Bristol — Cardiff service with a DC-3 on 29th April.

An easing in air transport regulation policy gave British Eagle the opportunity to compete with British European Airways on the London route, which they inaugurated on Monday, 4th November, 1963, with Britannia G-AOVT. British Eagle used the original terminal — 'terminal two' Renfrew! The service ceased on 19th February, 1965, due to government restrictions, according to the airline. It restarted on 5th July, with three flights daily including one which called at Liverpool. Starways, who had operated services between Liverpool and Renfrew, and Renfrew and Exeter, together with inclusive tours, were taken over, with their routes, by British Eagle in late 1963. However, in September, 1965, an announcement was made that British Eagle were to lose their Glasgow — London route, a decision which was successfully appealed. British United Airways, meanwhile, had expressed their wish to operate Renfrew to Gatwick and indeed, on 4th January, 1966, they inaugurated their 'Interjet' service with BAC One-Eleven, G-ASJJ — Renfrew's first pure-jet scheduled service though passenger complement had to be restricted due to the airport's limitations. British United Airways also, used the old terminal with its 1917/18 hangars — a link with flying's earliest days. Renfrew now had three airlines competing on the London route as its closure loomed nearer. On 7th January, 1966, the last Rolls Royce Merlin engine passed-out from 'D' Block, Hillington, just over the runway from Renfrew.

May 2nd, 1966, was the date chosen for the opening of Glasgow's new airport and duly, on the evening before, British European Airways ferried Heralds, 'WB and 'WD 'over the road' with Capt. Bob Chalmers in 'WB being the first to land. He wasn't the first to touch down at the new airport. An RAF Pembroke had done so by mistake on 26th April, and Capt. Ken Foster of Loganair had touched during checks for the Ministry of Aviation on the afternoon of the 1st in Piper Cherokee G-ATJV.

A thanksgiving service, led by the Airport Chaplain, Rev. Peter Houston, was held in one of the 'Lockheed' hangars on 17th April 1966. Among the congregation was Matron Miss Isobel Wares and three nurses from the

North West Airlines' DC-3, G-AGHO, on Isle of Man to Renfrew service, summer 1949.

The faithful DC-4, TF-RVH, 'Saga' of Iceland's Loftleidir at Renfrew, May, 1960.

Hunting-Clan DC-3, G-AMSJ, at Renfrew, summer, 1953.

TF-IST, 'Solfaxi', the 'Silver Horse', one of Flugfelag Islands' two DC-4s.

Cambrian Airways DC-3, G-AGHS.

DC-4, EI-AOR, of Aer Turas, 17th July, 1965.

Iceland's Flugfelag Islands DC-3, TF-ISA.

DC-4, G-ASPN, of British Eagle, 31st July, 1964.

Line-up of BEA's last DC-3, 'Pionairs' at Renfrew, April, 1962.

Rare visitor on 30th July, 1965, was this Indian Airlines' DC-4, VT-CZW.

The 'Super Dak' was a considerably modified DC-3 airframe which saw only limited service. The U.S. Navy however, used a number including 12437, a C-117 based at their Naval Air Facilities at West Malling, Kent. 2nd April, 1964.

The Danish operator, Flying Enterprise, also used DC-4Ms, such as OY-AAH, seen here at Renfrew in May, 1960.

One of Derby Aviations' former BOAC, R.R. Merlin powered Canadair DC-4Ms, G-ALHG, Renfrew, April, 1963.

Another Canadair DC-4M, G-ALHI, of Air Links visiting on 16th July, 1965.

Another Aviation Trader's Carvair, EC-AXI, of Aviaco at Renfrew on 12th May, 1965.

Caledonian Airways Douglas DC-6B, G-ASRZ, 25th July, 1964.

Flugfelag Islands became Icelandair, whose DC-6B, TF-ISC, 'Skytaxi' is shown landing on runway 08 at Renfrew.

DC-6B of the Norwegian Braathens SAFE, 14th April, 1965.

Iceland's long-haul airline was Loftleidir, which operated a transatlantic service from Renfrew, via Iceland from the mid-1950s. One of their DC-6Bs is shown landing over Renfrew Golf Course in 1963.

One of the Belgian airline Sabena's DC-6Bs, OO-CTH, at Renfrew, May,1963.

Lloyd International's DC-6B, G-ASTW, at Renfrew, 27th June, 1964.

One of the Dutch company, Martins Air Charter's DC-7Cs, PH-DSO, Renfrew, 21st June, 1964.

Lockheed L.049, Constellation, G-AHEL, (ex-BOAC) of Britannia Airways' predecessor Euravia, 1st August, 1964.

Skyways, L.149, Constellation, G-ARXE, 24th May, 1963.

Lockheed L.l049H, Super Constellation, N6919C, of the American, Flying Tiger Line, Renfrew, 14th July, 1963.

Hunting-Clan Air Transport's Viking, G-AGRW, at Renfrew in the early 1950s.

Handley Page Hermes 4, G-ALDA, of Air Safaris, 30th July, 1961.

One of the many small operators, which blossomed at the end of the fifties was Universal, whose Viking is seen here at Renfrew during May, 1960.

Bristol Freighter, G-AIME, of Silver City Airways.

Airspeed Ambassador, G-AMAH, of Dan-Air, 25th May, 1963.

Morton Air Services de Havilland Dove, G-ANAN, 9th July, 1963.

Unforgettable — the R.R. Merlin roar of Dan-Air's freighter Yorks, G-ANTI, April, 1961.

Dan-Air's Heron 1B, G-AOZM, 7th April, 1965.

Emerald Airways, Heron 1B, G-AOZN.

Curtiss C-46, Commando of Sweden's Transair, SE-CFD, 25th April, 1965.

Unusual visitor to Renfrew, a BEA 'Elizabethan' class Airspeed Ambassador, G-AMAF, 'Lord Howard of Effingham'.

Nord 262, LN-LME of Widerøe's, 18th June, 1963.

Sabena's Convair 440, OO-SCN at Renfrew, June, 1960.

From behind the iron-curtain, Czechoslavak, Ilyushin, Il-14, OK-BYO.

Polish airline, LOT's, Ilyushin, Il-18, SP-LSC, at Renfrew, September, 1967.

One of the Ministry of Aviation's, Civil Aviation Flying Units' Doves, G-ANOV, 28th April, 1966 — no doubt involved in checking out the new Glasgow Airport, at Abbotsinch, prior to its opening a few days later.

One of the very few Percival Presidents, (Civil Pembroke), G-APMO, of the Ministry of Aviation, 21st June, 1964.

Royal Air Force Rescue Westland Whirlwind HAR 10, XJ723, 7th June, 1964.

British Eagle resurrected the old terminal at Renfrew, when they began their London — Glasgow services in 1963.

Britannia Airways, Bristol Britannia 102, G-ANBA, 17th July, 1965.

Whilst a British United Airways DC-3 takes-off, British Eagle Viscount V.739, G-ATDU, 'City of Liverpool' taxies in, 30th July, 1965.

Liverpool based Starways' Viscount V.708, G-ARIR, ON 11th August, 1962.

Starways, having been taken over by British Eagle, display their name on one of the latter's Viscounts V.701, G-AMOO, 'City of Birmingham', in 1964, at the old terminal.

*Channel Airways Viscount V.70l,
G-ALWF, 16th June, 1965.*

*Cambrian Airways Viscount V.70l,
G-AMOP, 5th January, 1963.*

*British United's Viscount V.708,
G-ARBY, at the old terminal.*

*Icelandair's first Viscount V.759, TF-
ISN, 'Gullfaxi'. The name was originally
given to the famous DC-4, TF-ISE.*

Fred Olsen's Viscount V.779, LN-FOK.

*Another user of the Handley Page Herald
was British United Airways — G-APWJ,
is seen at Renfrew, July, 1963.*

Loganair's first Britten Norman Islander, G-AVRA, with one of their Piper Aztecs, 1966.

Loganair's Piper Tri-Pacer, G-ARHV.

G-ASFL, Piper Cherokee 180, of Loganair.

Capt. Duncan McIntosh, 'Captain Mac', of Loganair, with Aztec, G-ASYB.

Loganair's first Piper Aztec, G-ARMH, in front of their hangar at Renfrew, May, 1962.

The newly established Glasgow Flying Club's Bölkow Junior, G-ATRI, at Renfrew, 23rd April, 1966.

Big Piper, Cherokee 6, G-ATJV, of Loganair, April, 1966.

Caledonian Flying Services' Thruxton Jackaroo, Tiger Moth conversion, G-AOIT, 28th June, 1963.

Jimmy Logan, one of Scotland's great entertainers, with his Miles Gemini, G-AJWC, which he flew from Renfrew during the early 1960s.

The Automobile Association's Piper Apache, G-APZE, 14th July, 1963.

One of the popular Piaggio P.166 executive aircraft of the early 1960s, G-APYP, of the Nuclear Power Group, October, 1962.

Robert Bluck's Gemini, G-AKEI, which also flew from Renfrew, 12th May, 1961.

Philips' Beech E.18s, PH-LPS, a regular Renfrew visitor, 20th June, 1961.

Beagle Terrier, G-ASOI, owned by Wg. Cdr. Jock Dalgleish and used by the Edinburgh Flying Club, 31st July, 1965.

Ferranti's Grumman Mallard amphibian, G-ASCS, 22nd September, 1962.

Beagle 206 owned by Rolls-Royce, G-ASWJ, 30th December, 1965.

Davy Ashmore's Beech Queen Air, G-ARFF, at Renfrew, 4th March, 1962.

Rutherglen Popular Flying Association Group's ill-fated Piel Emeraude, G-ASKR. The aircraft subsequently crashed and burnt-out on take-off at Couplaw Farm, Strathaven.

AAH . . . de Havilland

Echo of the past! One of the last two de Havilland Dragons on the British Register, G-ADDI, at Renfrew, 27th June, 1965.

Hunting Surveys' de Havilland Rapide, G-AIYR, 16th May, 1964.

Rare, de Havilland Dragonfly, G-ANYK, at Renfrew, 9th June, 1961.

Rolls-Royce's de Havilland Heron 2D, G-AOTI, another regular, 22nd May, 1964.

B.S.R.'s executive Dove, G-ASMG.

Successor to B.S.R.'s Dove was executive jet, de Havilland 125, G-ASSM, of B.S.R., a regular visitor, 6th April, 1965.

Beech H.l8s, G-ASNX, of the Cameron Iron Works, 20th August, 1965.

S.T.C.'s executive DC-3, G-AJRY, 7th August, 1965.

Whisky Company's Chivas' North American Sabreliner, N2275W, 14th May, 1965.

Renfrew's first civil jet transport movement — Iberia's Sud-Aviation Caravelle, EC-ARI 'Albeniz', April, 1962.

British United Airways inaugurated the first pure-jet scheduled services between Glasgow and London in January, 1966. Here, their BAC One-Eleven, G-ASJH, is seen taking-off.

Southern General Hospital, one of whom, Sister Jean Stalker, had flown by then, 85 Air Ambulance missions.

The last scheduled air service to leave Renfrew on the morning of the 2nd, was British European Airways' Vanguard G-APEN *Valiant*, bound for London. It flew past in salute at 0733 hours. One aircraft remained at Renfrew, minus wings, the Thruxton Jackaroo G-AOIT of Caledonian Flying Services.

Soon the 08 runway almost became the M8 motorway and new housing schemes were built on much of the old airport's site by Renfrew Town Council. To safeguard their interests, a compulsory purchase order, which had been raised by the Ministry of Aviation in 1960, covering the greater part of the airport, had been withdrawn as a result of the Council giving the Ministry a 99 year lease. Their wartime requisition ended that year, as did their interest on the airport's closure. Glasgow's new airport at Abbotsinch was successfully opened on 2nd May, 1966, and officially opened by H.M. The Queen on 27th June.

On 23rd October, 1966, Capt. David Barclay, MBE, unveiled a cairn, dedicated to the memory of the crew who lost their lives on Islay in 1957, whilst answering an Air Ambulance call — Capt. T.N. (Paddy) Calderwood; Radio Officer Hugh McGinley; and Nursing Sister Jean Kennedy. Sited appropriately at the junction of Newmains and Sandy Roads, it is a fitting memorial to them and to all the crews of the Scottish Air Ambulance Service from Midland & Scottish Air Ferries, Northern and Scottish Airways, Scottish Airways, British European Airways, British Airways and Loganair, together with the silver winged volunteer flying nurses of Glasgow's Southern General Hospital.

Thus a great, intriguing and sometimes frustrating chapter in the aviation history of this country ended and another began. This account has mentioned only a few of the men and women who made it a success — James G. Weir, A.C.H. MacLean, Provost D.K. Michie, John Sword, Winnie Drinkwater. Bill Mann, Bill Cumming and Jock Bain, David Barclay, George Nicholson of Scottish Airways and Robert McKean and Eric Starling. Among airport officials, Messrs. Millen, Oakley, Waldron, Murray and Hendry. The author recalls as a 'spotter' that even among that stern bunch of men, the airport police there were kindly souls, who would turn a blind eye to his illegal sorties among the hangars, seeking out details for his drawings. Renfrew was widely known as a 'friendly airport'. Let that be its epitaph and an aspiration for its successor.

Mrs. Anne Heads and her new baby — the 10 000th customer of the Air Ambulance service, January, 1973, with John McDermid, the first — May, 1933.

A.1950/60s Air Ambulance sequence.

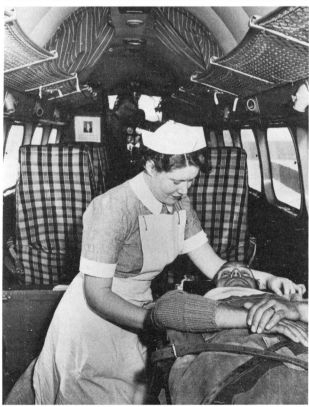

The first of two de Havilland Heron 1Bs are cermoniously saluted by the irrepressible, Capt. David Barclay, flying a Dragon Rapide.

Capt. Eric Starling, pioneer commercial pilot and BEA's Flight Manager, Scotland, from 1949 to 1968, thereafter, in charge of Scottish Air Ambulance Service until he retired in 1971.

The Scottish Air Ambulance service, by now run by Scottish Airways using Spartan Cruisers, 1938/39.

Captain David Barclay, MBE, unveils the memorial cairn to the Scottish Air Ambulance Service, 23rd October, 1966.

110

G L A S G O W —
T H E   N E W   A I R P O R T

by Alan Carlaw

H.M.S SANDERLING	(ABBOTTINC
24 1/6'50 FAIREY FIREFLY I	R.N. DK483
HAWKER SEA FURY II	R.N. VR972
FAIREY FIREFLY I	R.N. PP936
HAWKER SEA FURY II	R.N. VW573
FAIREY FIREFLY I	R.N. DV123
SUPERMARINE SPITFIRE 21 (RAI·F)	R.A.F LA250
SUPERMARINE SPITFIRE 22 (LO·B)	R.A.F PK368
D.H.82 TIGER MOTH (5ASE VARSMROV·B)	R.A.F N9272
D.H.82 TIGER MOTH (AUG·C)	R.A.F N6719
D.H.82 TIGER MOTH (AUG·A)	R.A.F DF112
D.H.82 TIGER MOTH (AUG·D)	R.A.F N9205
D.H.82 TIGER MOTH (RCM·D)	R.A.F DF637
SUPERMARINE SPITFIRE 21 (RAI·J)	R.A.F LA265
SUPERMARINE SEAFIRE (Cocoon)	R.N. PR366
FAIREY FIREFLY 4	R.N. VG985
FAIREY FIREFLY I (273)	R.N. PP405
SUPERMARINE SPITFIRE 22 (LO·D)	R.A.F PK349
FAIREY FIREFLY I	R.N MB728
FAIREY FIREFLY I	R.N. MB720
HAWKER SEA FURY II	R.N VT5946
HAWKER SEA FURY (Cocoon)	R.N. EK736
HAWKER SEA FURY II	R.N. AAA
HAWKER SEA FURY 10	R.N. TF960

30 SEPTEMBER 1955 ABBOTSINCH			
13878	H19A	USAF RESCUE	
XB361	AVENGER	FAA	Cocooned
XB372	AVENGER	FAA	"
XB384	AVENGER	FAA	"
XB321	AVENGER	FAA	"
VZ657	SEA HORNET	FAA	"
VZ659	SEA HORNET	FAA	"
VR858	SEA HORNET	FAA	"
WV863	SEA HAWK	FAA	c/163
VA879 ✓	MOSSI 73	FAA	Cocoon VR879.
VA880 ✓	MOSSI 73	FAA	"
✝V 954 ✓	MOSSI T3	FAA	"
TV 964 ✓	MOSSI T3	FAA	"
VT 607 ✓	MOSSI T3	FAA	"
VT 619 ✓	MOSSI T3	FAA	"
XB378	AVENGER	FAA	
XB301	AVENGER	FAA	
XE450	SEA HAWK	FAA	
WM911	SEA HAWK	FAA	
XB305	AVENGER	FAA	"294" SCRAPED
WP289	ATTACKER	FAA	
HG709	DOMINIE	FAA AC/901	
WK480	METEOR	RAF 602SQN	
VP965	DEVON	RAF	
RENFREW			
23008	SABRE 5	RCAF	
23087	SABRE 5	RCAF	
23115	SABRE 5	RCAF	

Glasgow Airport opened for commercial traffic on 2 May 1966 but the area had been a flying site for more than thirty years prior to that date. Abbot's Inch, some 700 acres of ground between the Black and White Cart rivers, was said to have been gifted to Paisley Abbey in the early 13th century although it may have been the home of monks under St Mirren at an even earlier date. It was not until 1932 that the area was considered for aeronautical use when Abbotsinch was surveyed as an alternative airfield for No.602(City of Glasgow) Squadron of the Auxiliary Air Force which was short of space at nearby Renfrew aerodrome. The Squadron moved in on 20 January 1933 and remained there until 7 October 1939 by which time it had been mobilised for full time duty in the RAF and moved to the east coast of Scotland for defence duties.

Other RAF units using the airfield before the war included 21 and 34 Squadrons with Hinds, 269 Squadron with Ansons and 607 Squadron with Gladiators. No.51 Elementary & Reserve Flying Training School (E & RFTS) opened in August 1939 with Tiger Moths but closed early in September and other units using the Station included: No.2 Coastal Patrol Flight with Tiger Moths; 816, 818, 819 and 824 Naval Air Squadrons with Swordfish; the Torpedo Training Unit using Swordfish, Beaufort and Botha aircraft; 801 Squadron with Skuas and 309 Squadron with Lysanders. 807 Squadron and 800Y Squadron, both with Fulmars, were present in 1941 and other users were: 1441 Flight with Lysanders and Ansons; 239 and 225 Squadrons with Mustangs and Hurricanes and 892 Naval Air Squadron with Wildcats. With the continuing use by Fleet Air Arm squadrons it was not surprising that, on 11 August 1943, control of the Station was passed to the Royal Navy and HMS Sanderling, as it became known, was commissioned on 20 September that year. In Fleet Air Arm use it served as an aircraft maintenance yard and training station and was home to a number of FAA squadrons flying Avengers, Hellcats, Wildcats, Sea Hurricanes, Seafires, Swordfish and Barracuda.

After the war RNAS Abbotsinch served as a repair base for fighter aircraft from British, American and Canadian carriers and was later used for fitting and testing new aircraft as well as inspecting, modifying and storing older ones. During this time several 'lodger' units arrived, most significantly No.602 Squadron which reformed with Spitfires on 11 June 1946 although the first aircraft for the Squadron was a Harvard T.2B (KF374). The first Spitfire, a FR.Mk.14E (TP236), arrived on 22 October, one of five such examples, but the main equipment was the F.21 the first two of which arrived on 10 April 1947 (LA193 & LA250). These were supplemented by some F.22s in the following year and were flown until replaced with Vampires in January 1951. 602 was joined by No.1830 Squadron RNVR on 15 August 1947, initially equipped with Seafire F.XVIIs and Firefly FR.1s which, in turn, gave way to other marks of Firefly, Sea Fury T.20 and, in 1953/55, Anson, Sea Prince, Sea Balliol and Avenger AS.5s. No.1967 Flight from 666 Squadron, Royal Auxiliary Air Force, arrived from Scone on 5 December 1952 with Auster AOP aircraft for army co-operation duties. Also present were the Magisters and Tiger Moths of Glasgow University Air Squadron which formed in 1946.

The notoriously boggy conditions of the ground eventually necessitated the laying of permanent tarmac runways in place of the metal track and the airfield was closed in 1950 for this work to be done although 602 Squadron had by then moved back to its birthplace at Renfrew in July 1949. The University Air Squadron, whose tail-skid Tiger Moths could not use the metal track runways, had temporarily re-equipped with Magisters went to Scone in 1950 and the RNVR's 1830 Squadron operated from Donibristle. While at Donibristle 1830 formed an offshoot, No.1830A Squadron, on 1 October 1952 as part of the RNVR's Scottish Air Division. It shared the parent unit's aircraft and returned to Abbotsinch with 1830 on 1 November 1952 but acquired its own identity as 1843 Squadron on 28 March 1953 and flew Avengers from November 1955 before disbanding in 1957. The airfield re-opened in late 1952 and the major units slowly returned although 602 was not in place until April 1954.

A run-down in military aviation led to the disbandment of all Auxiliary flying units in the UK on 10 March 1957 although flying had been forbidden from 6 January. The City lost its famous Fighter Squadron together with the RNVR's 1830 & 1843 Squadrons and No.1967 AOP Flight. Another piece of West of Scotland aviation history occurred in March 1944 when No.4 Gliding School formed at Paisley. The actual details of this unit are vague but it is known that it was located at RNAS Abbotsinch by May 1945 and renamed No.663 Volunteer Gliding School on 24 November 1955. It flew Sedbergh and Mk.3 Gliders until disbanding in September 1963.

A general reduction in size of the Fleet Air Arm in the early 1960s rendered the Station surplus to operational requirements and it closed on 31 October 1963 with the White Ensign being lowered for the last time at noon on that day but by then its future had been soundly secured with the Ministry of Civil Aviation acting as custodians during the next two and a half years.

The development of commercial aviation in the 1950s had seen larger and faster aircraft come into service and it was soon realised that the airport for Glasgow at Renfrew had reached its limit of expansion and an alternative had to be found. On 14 November 1960 it was announced that Abbotsinch would be developed as the new airport for Glasgow and the City's Corporation would assume responsibility for its operation although the idea had by then been public knowledge for more than a year. The cost of conversion and new building was £4.2m and the main contractor was John Laing Construction Ltd.

Under the control of Ronald A. Read DFC, the Airport's first Director, services

RNVR Scottish Air Division, Firefly, Abbotsinch.

Abbotsinch and Renfrew from the air, early 1930s.

The originial RAF airfield at Abbotsinch, 1933/34 — the Hawker Harts and Avro Tutors of 602 Squadron, can be seen.

The new Glasgow Airport at Abbotsinch, during construction.

were transferred from Renfrew to the new Glasgow Airport at 0800hrs on 2 May 1966 and the first commercial flight to land was a BEA Viscount, G-AOYP, at 0700hrs from Edinburgh. Piloted by Captain Eric Starling, the Airline's Scottish flight manager, the Viscount carried 64 members of the staff of Sir Basil Spence, Glover and Ferguson, architects of the airport. The aircraft had earlier flown from Renfrew to Turnhouse to collect its passengers. Various aircraft had been flown in the previous day in readiness for the first outgoing flights with BEA Heron, G-ANXA, being the first actual movement of the day. The first scheduled flight to land was BEA Herald, G-APWB carrying 41 fare-paying passengers from Aberdeen and Edinburgh, touched down at 0821hrs but the new airport had been unofficially 'opened' five days earlier when an RAF Pembroke landed mistaking the runway for that of nearby Renfrew!

On 2 May there were a number of notable 'firsts' as BEA inaugurated its twice daily jet service to London with Comet 4B, G-ARJN, and British Eagle operated a jet proving flight with BAC 1-11, G-ATTP.

The 'official' opening was carried out by Her Majesty The Queen on 27 June. July saw the first visit by a VC10 (British United's G-ASIX) and also by a Trident One (BEA's G-ARPD) although regular services with this latter type did not begin until 3 April 1967. British Eagle introduced its Dundee-Glasgow service on 2 July 1966 flying a Dove, G-AROI appropriately named 'Eaglet', and a Lockheed Constellation of ACE Scotland, G-ASYF, was based at the airport from 14 July until this operation ceased after only two months. Emerald Airways opened its Londonderry route on 16 September with a Heron, G-ALZL. BEA's last commercial flight by a Herald, G-APWD, was flown on 31 October when Captain Burnett arrived from Islay and Campbeltown at 1736hrs. The airport's one millionth passenger was handled on 20 December 1966.

The first BEA scheduled Trident One service was flown on 3 April 1967 by G-ARPT. By 1 May 1967 the airport had handled 654 different aircraft, 1.5 million passengers and 34 000 aircraft movements and it is interesting to note that even at this early stage of development it was seeking trans-Atlantic services. Iberia started its Barcelona service with a Caravelle (EC-ARJ) on 2 June and American Flyers joined Wardair in operating flights across the Atlantic — the former's first service was operated by Lockheed Electra N122US. The following day saw the first visit of Icelandair's Boeing 727 TF-FIE. An 'old friend' returned on 19 March 1968 when the DC-3 G-ALYF (ex-BEA Pioneer 'Pionair') arrived by road for use by the fire section. The first visit of a Trident Two, BEA's G-AVFD, was on 2 June and KLM introduced a freight service to Amsterdam in September using DC-9s -first service by PH-DNO. The first visit of a Boeing 737 — now a common sight — occured on 14 October with the arrival of Britannia Airways' G-AVRM.

Another significant event occurred in October 1968 with the formation of the West of Scotland Flying Club at Glasgow Airport under the auspices of the Edinburgh Flying Club. With two Cessna 150s, drawn from G-AVEL, G-AVTN, G-AVVL and G-AWPP, and Cessna 172G G-ATSL the Club flourished under Chief Flying Instructor Ian Cooper. This book's author learned to fly there under the guidance of Peter Turner, a part-time instructor.

SAS introduced a service to Copenhagen on 2 November with Caravelles (first service by SE-DAG' *Dag Viking'*) but four days later British Eagle went into liquidation with Cambrian taking over the route to Liverpool. The return of a 'military presence' occurred 8 November when the Universities of Glasgow & Strathclyde Air Squadron moved in with their five Chipmunks from Scone. Since then this unit has attracted a variety of service aircraft to the airport. The first visit of a Handley Page Jetstream, G-ATXJ, was on 17 February 1969 — it is interesting to note that the Jetstream is now a highly successful product from British Aerospace's Prestwick factory.

Another first visit, that of a Convair CV-990 (Spantax's EC-BJD) was on 23 May and two months later, on 20 July many thousands of miles from Glasgow, another first visit took place when, at 2118hrs BST, Apollo Eleven's lunar module, *'Eagle'*, touched down on the moon. The withdrawal of KLM's services through Prestwick in 1969 enabled that airline to establish a twice weekly service from Glasgow to Amsterdam beginning on 3 November using DC-9s -first service by PH-DNR. Although a BOAC Boeing 747, G-AWNC, had made a low overshoot on 1 August 1970, the largest aircraft to land that year was a KLM DC 8-63, PH-DEK, on 11 September.

The summer inclusive tour business was increasing with flights by Laker, Dan-Air, British Midland, Inex Adria, Tarom, Bulair, Britannia, Channel, Iberia, British United and Trans Europa using types as varied as Russian IL 18s to Comets and Caravelles. On 7 June 1971 a low overshoot was carried out by Lockheed L1011 TriStar N301EA prior to flypasts of Rolls-Royce factories at Hillington and East Kilbride. On 13 November Loftleidir introduced DC-8s in place of its CL44s — the first service was by TF-LLK.

December witnessed the retiral of Captain Eric Starling, BEA's Flight Manager in Scotland from 1949 to 1968 and thereafter in charge of the Air Ambulance Service. In the same month BEA's Scottish Division was renamed the Scottish Airways Division with the name 'Scottish Airways' being carried on the two Herons and some Viscounts. Robert McKean, OBE, was appointed Chairman of the Division having been with BEA management in Scotland since 1948. He retired on 30 June 1973.

On 4 April 1972 Lufthansa launched the Frankfurt — Manchester — Glasgow service with Boeing 737 D-ABEO and on the 26 April the RAF's Red Arrows Gnats gave a spectacular display on their pre-Season press tour. Such was the excitement and to some the disturbance, created that the Team were prevented by court injunction from flying three days later during the University Air Squadron's Scone Trophy competition. The airport had its first visits of 'wide bodied' jets — Lockheed TriStar N305EA on 17 September and Laker DC-10 G-AZZC on 24 November. During the year 'British Airways' was formed by the amalgamation of BOAC and BEA together with its subsidiaries Northeast and Cambrian. The name 'British Airways' was used from 1 September 1973 although the routes were not integrated until 1974.

Abbotsinch, Empire Air Day, 29th May, 1937.
Vickers Vildebeeste I — K28l2, 42 Squadron, Donibristle.

The first Spitfires — 602 Squadron at Abbotsinch, just at the beginning of the Second World War.

Avro Ansons of 269, General Reconaissance Squadron, Abbotsinch at the outbreak of war.

A Blackburn Botha and Fairey Swordfish at Abbotsinch, 1940.

Spitfire F.21, LA198, RAI-G, at Abbotsinch in early 1949. It was preserved at RAF Leuchars in its 602 Squadron markings, during 1986-87.

Scottish Air Division, RNVR Firefly A.S.6, WD858, 220/AC. Summer? 1955 at Abbotsinch.

Grumman Avenger, XB397, of the Scottish Air Division, RNVR at Abbotsinch, 1956.

The dump at Abbotsinch, late 1950s — what would we give now for Sea Mosquitos and Sea Hornets!

Abbotsinch, late 1950s — the Avenger and Skyraider hangar was conveniently situated, for spotters, next to the road.

The 'Attacker' hangar, on the other side of the road, next to the river.

Vickers Supermarine Attacker — Gate guardian at RNAS Abbotsinch, HMS Sanderling, prior to its becoming Glasgow Airport (pre 1963).
This aircraft went to the Fleet Air Arm Museum at RNAS Yeovilton.

Ace Scottish Lockheed L.749 Constellation, G-ASYF, at Abbotsinch during an engine change — a very short-lived operation.

With Scottish Airways titles, BEA Viscount, G-AOJF.

Formerly with BOAC, Comet 4, G-APDD, in service with Dan Air.

Stalwart performer on BEA's, then British Airways' Glasgow-London services. HS Trident I, G-ARPI.

Britannias were used by a number of charter operators in the '60s and early '70s. G-AOVC belonged to Donaldson International.

Caledonian BUA, BAC One-Eleven, G-AWYS.

One of Britannia Airways first Boeing 737s, G-AVRN.

Dan Air's HS748, G-ARAY.

'Smokey Joe', Icelandair's Boeing 727, TF-FIE. The new 'Gullfaxi'.

The 'Red Arrows' at Glasgow Airport, April 1972.

West of Scotland Flying Club's Cessna 150, G-AWPP.

Launch of 'the book Glasgow's Own' at Glasgow Airport (Abbotsinch), Monday, 14th December, 1987. In front of Tornado F.3, ZE205 'AA' of 229 OCU (65 Reserve Squadron) are:

L. to R.:. Alastair Grant, ?, Johnny Lake, Alastair Young, ?, Glen Niven, Donald Jack, J.B. Murray, Randall Phillips, Alex Bowman, Marcus Robinson, Tommy Love, Jim Johnston, Jack Daly, Jack Forrest, Hector MacLean.

In Front: Alan Carlaw, George Pinkerton, Dugald Cameron.

Mrs Ann Heads became the 10,000th Air Ambulance passenger on 8 January 1973 when she arrived at Glasgow from Ardbeg on Islay. When she returned home she was met by Mr John McDermid — the service's first passenger! BA Viscount 802 (G-AOHI) crashed into Ben More on 19 January while on an engineering test flight from Glasgow with the loss of all on board. A Short Skyliner, G-AZYW, arrived on 8 March heralding the end of the Heron era. Court Line's TriStar, G-BAAA, gave a demonstration flight on 27 March and 31 March saw the last BA Heron service from Barra & Tiree. The Herons, G-ANXA/B, were replaced by Skyliners, G-AZYW & G-BAIT. A British Airways Boeing 747, G-AWNM, made two ILS runs — one low overshoot and one touch-and-go making the first — albeit brief — visit of the type on 10 May. Lufthansa withdrew from the Manchester — Frankfurt service at the end of October but British Island Airways introduced a new service to Dublin on 2 November using Heralds in competition with Aer Lingus. The end of the year also saw the resignation of the airport's first director who left to take up an appointment in the Middle East.

New equipment in the shape of Prestwick-built Scottish Aviation Bulldog T.1s (XX559, 560, 557 & 611) replaced the Chipmunks of the University Air Squadron in March 1974 and in May Swissair started a four times weekly DC-9 freighter service Zurich — Glasgow — Manchester — Zurich. British Airways announced the pending withdrawal of the Skyliner aircraft and introduction of HS 748s and the transfer of some services to Loganair. Agreement was reached between Glasgow Corporation and British Airports Authority on 6 January 1975 for transfer of ownership with effect from 1 April. The first visit of a Super VC10, British Airways' G-ASGF, was on 11 January and the following day BA introduced its London 'Shuttle' service with Trident One aircraft — the first inbound was G-ARPC. The Loganair Dundee service was suspended on 30 May due to continuing losses. On 10 July the first HS 748, G-BCOE 'Glen Livet', was delivered for BA's Scottish routes. The first passenger service by a Boeing 747 was operated by Alitalia's I-DEMO on 24 October.

12 May 1976 was probably the busiest day ever at Glasgow Airport. The European Cup final between Bayern Munich and St Etienne played at Hampden Park attracted no less than 12 Caravelles, 7 DC-8s, 4 Vanguards, 3 Boeing 727s, 3 Boeing 747s, 2 BAC 1-11s and one each A-300, Boeing 707, DC-9, Herald, Trident Two and VFW-614 plus 27 light executive aircraft on the airfield by kick-off. An additional 55 airliners and 11 light aircraft used Prestwick and Edinburgh airports!

Duncan MacIntosh brought the Miles Student G-APLK to Glasgow on 21 December — the aircraft was seen as a cheap jet trainer.

A £2 million extension to the international (east) terminal began in June and was scheduled to be complete in 18 months. On 1 November Air Anglia introduced a service to Humberside and Norwich using PA-31 Navajos. The SAS route licence dispute between UK and Denmark saw the Glasgow — Copenhagen licence revoked but the airline revived its Copenhagen — Prestwick — New York licence and operated a part service from Copenhagen

1977

April. Plans unveiled for a new use of 1954 Renfrew Terminal Buildings — shopping and leisure development proposed — came to nothing and regrettably this quite significant building was eventually demolished, a Tesco superstore being built on the site. Little now remains to remind the passerby of this cradle of Scottish flying. Some of the roads in the new housing estate however, perpetuate something of the place's history — 'Viscount Way', 'Britannia Avenue' and, appropriately, the commemorative cairn to the Scottish Air Ambulance Service. The Cemetery, however, maintains its timeless presence though most of the ships and cranes which were the other readily identifiable features of Renfrew are sadly much reduced in number.

1978

8 Jan. Dan-Air 'Shetland Shuttle' at its peak — no less than nine different HS748s noted.

3 April. British Airways start Glasgow — Paris, Monday — Friday; Glasgow — Birmingham — Milan, Monday — Friday; and Glasgow — Copenhagen, Monday, Wednesday and Friday — the latter in competition with Scandinavian Air Services and Icelandair.

British Midland Airways celebrate 21 years on Glasgow — Derby route.

2 May. Air Westward start weekday Glasgow — Exeter service using Ce404.

13 Dec. Burnthills start weekday Glasgow — Fort William helicopter service using Jet Ranger.

Air Anglia increased Glasgow — Teesside — Humberside service.

Summer ITs — Air Malta B720; Aviaco DC8/DC9; B.Cal. BAC1-11; Balkan Tu154; Inex Adria DC9; LOT Tu134/IL18; Dan-Air Comet; Britannia B737; British Airways Trident 3; Tarom B707/Tu154.

1979

1 May. Air Westward cease trading — Glasgow — Exeter route passed to BIA then Air UK, latter using EMB110 from 5th December.

MAC C5A Galaxy 69-019 brought in United States Navy rescue submarine, 'Deep Submergence Rescue Vehicle' from San Diego, California, for an exercise. The aircraft arrived from North Island NAS, California, and was accompanied by C141A 66-169 which came from McGuire AFC, New Jersey.

13 May. Return leg using C5A 69-008 to Dover AFB, Delaware and C141A 64-647 to McGuire AFB, New Jersey.

25 July. Final meeting of Scottish Flying Club at 2 West Regent Street, Glasgow. George Pinkerton, its last Chairman, presiding. Couplaw Farm, Strathaven, which had been bought by the Scottish Flying Club in late1963 and used by various flying and gliding groups/ clubs was gifted to the RAF Benevolent Fund, who continued its use for flying and particularly, gliding. The Universities of Glasgow and Strathclyde Gliding Club being the main users. Other remaining monies were donated to Erskine Hospital with £1000 going to Linburn Hospital for the war-blinded.

16 Oct. Expansion of mail flights with Air Ecosse operating Glasgow — Liverpool and Luton

Air UK suspended Glasgow — Exeter services — late in year?

Summer ITs — Britannia B737; Air Malta B720; Inex Adria DC9; B.Cal. ABC1-11; Balkan Tu154; Dan-air B727/BAC1-11; Aviaco DC9; British Midland DC9. Tarom B707/I162/Tu154; Spantax CV990; LOT Tu134; JAT B707/B727; Aviogenex Tu134; Aeroflot Tu134.

to Prestwick with DC-9 aircraft. In 1978 the Dan-Air 'Shetland Shuttle' was at its peak and on 8 January no less than nine different HS 748s were noted. In April 1978 a number of new services to Europe were introduced when British Airways launched flights to Paris (Mon — Fri), Birmingham — Milan (Mon — Fri) and Copenhagen (Mon, Wed, Fri) — the latter in competition with SAS and Icelandair. British Midland celebrated 21 years on the Derby route and Air Westward started a service to Exeter using a Cessna 404. In December Burnthills Aviation started a weekday service to Fort William using a Jet Ranger helicopter.

On 1 May 1979 Air Westward ceased trading and the Exeter route passed to British Island Airways and on 5 December to Air UK who employed EMB-110s. Outsized visitors in May this year included USAF C-5A Galaxys (69-0019 & 69-0008) bringing and returning a US Navy deep sea rescue submarine for an exercise in the Clyde estuary. Support was provided in both directions by C-141B Starlifters (66-0169 & 64-0647). The final meeting of the Scottish Flying Club took place on 25 July at 2 West Regent Street, Glasgow with George Pinkerton, its last Chairman, presiding. Couplaw Farm at Strathaven, which had been bought by the Club in 1963 and since used by various flying and gliding groups, was gifted to the RAF Benevolent Fund who continued its use for flying and, particularly, gliding — the Universities of Glasgow & Strathclyde Gliding Club being the main user. Other monies were donated to Erskine Hospital with £1,000 going to Linburn Hospital for the war-blinded. October 1980 saw an increase of mail flights to Liverpool and Luton by Air Ecosse and, not surprisingly, Air UK withdrew from the Exeter service in December.

Fog at Heathrow caused three British Airways Boeing 747s to divert on 3 January 1981 but the year was to witness the withdrawal of the Icelandair Copenhagen service in May and BA to the same destination in December. Burnthills began a helicopter service to Rothesay and Lochgilphead while Eastern took over the Humberside service with PA-31 Navajos, and later Short 330s, with Casair operating the service to Teesside with PA-31s. The main attraction of 1981 was, however, the first visit of Concorde when British Airways' G-BOAG arrived on 11 October.

In 1982 British Airways flew four "Farewell to the Viscount" charter flights to Kirkwall on 27/28 March using 806s G-AOYL/M/O & G-APIM although the last schedule flight was not until 8 May — BA5721 from Inverness with G-AOYM. Icelandair resumed its Copenhagen service on 2 April and later that month British Airways re-organised its Scottish operations to form Highlands Division based at Glasgow Airport under Gerry Devine when new unique operating practices were introduced to safeguard the continuance of the airline's long established Scottish operations. Services were now geared round the HS/BAe.748. British Midland won its appeal and began services to London Heathrow with six flights daily Monday to Friday and four at weekends using DC-9s. The first southbound service was on 25 October was with G-BMAB. Later in the year SAS withdrew the Copenhagen freighter service.

On 5 January 1983 BCal named its BAC 1-11 Srs.515, G-AZPZ, *'City of Glasgow'* at a ceremony at the airport and the first visit of a Boeing 757, BA's G-BIKB *'Windsor Castle'*, on 5 February heralded the introduction of this type to 'Shuttle' operations on 11 February. On 23 February Trident One G-ARPP, once familiar to Glasgow passengers, made its last flight as 'Shuttle 6F' and was then delivered to the airport's fire service where it still remains on the eastern side of the airfield. The first regular 'wide bodied' service was operated throughout the summer by BCal DC-10s to Palma and Ibiza. On 7 June NASA Boeing 747 (N905NA) with Space Shuttle *'Enterprise'* atop made a low pass at the airport and then overflew East Kilbride. British Airways introduced the 'Super Shuttle' services to London on 30 August and no less than three Concordes, G-BOAA/B/D, were together at Glasgow in celebration. Although not strictly at Glasgow Airport an event took place nearby on 22 October when Marshal of the Royal Air Force Lord Cameron opened the 602(City of Glasgow) Squadron museum adjacent to No.2175(Rolls-Royce) Squadron Air Training Corps headquarters at Hillington.

The first visit of an A-310 Airbus, BCal's G-BKWU, occured on 21 March 1984. Metropolitan tookover the Leeds/Bradford route from Dan-Air on 26 March and later started a Newcastle service in association with BCal. March also saw the suspension of Burnthills helicopter services although a limited operation to Rothesay was resumed in mid August. The airport's first regular Boeing 747 service started in May when Aviaco introduced Iberia aircraft to Tenerife — first movement was with EC-DIA. Loganair began services to Manchester on 25 September and on 1 October Air UK tookover the BCal Newcastle — Amsterdam route using BIA BAC 1-11s until its leased Fokker F.28 was delivered. A British Airtours B.747, G-BDXL *' City of Windsor'*, diverted in from Prestwick on 18 October due to crosswinds and then routed direct to Toronto. BA Highlands Division took delivery of its first BAe.748 Super 2B, G-HDBA *'Glen Esk'* , on 13 December.

The first visit of a Boeing 767, Britannia Airways' G-BKPW, was on 27 March1985 while the last Trident flight was on 29 December when Trident Three G-AWZO operated 'Shuttle 7L'. Malinair commenced opertions to Carrickfinn in December with two BN-2 Islanders. The opening of the News International newspaper printing plant at Kinning Park in Glasgow on 26 January 1986 has lead to a significant increase in night newspaper delivery flights. March saw delivery flights of CASA 212s — four for the Venezuelan Navy and five for the Mexican Navy — emphasising Glasgow Airport's increasing North Atlantic delivery traffic. Lufthansa introduced a service to Dusseldorf on 1 April with DLT EMB.120s and Icelandair resumed the Reykjavik — Vagar(Faroes) — Glasgow service). On 24 October Malinair took delivery of a leased Do.228 PH-SDO (later registered G-MLDO) pending the arrival of its own aircraft, G-CFIN, in January 1987.

Air Ecosse suspended operations on 19 January 1987 but in March Chieftain Airways took delivery of two HS.748s, G-GLAS & G-EDIN, for services to Brussels and a Be.200 (G-BHVX) for the Hamburg route. The airline commenced operations on 29 March but, sadly, went into receivership on 13

1981

3 Jan. Three British Airways B747s divert from Heathrow due to fog.

24 March. Runway 06/24 becomes 05/23 due to magnetic variation movement.

29 May. Icelandair cease flying Glasgow — Copenhagen.

11 Oct. First visit by Concorde to Glasgow — G-BOAG.

26 December. Eastern take over Glasgow — Humberside with PA31 going up to Short 330 while Casair take over Glasgow — Teeside with PA31.

Burnthills started Glasgow — Rothesay and Lochgilphead, helicopter service.

British Airways pull out of Glasgow — Copenhagen and announce major shake-up which will lead to Highlands Division.

Air Ecosse operate Glasgow — Liverpool three times each weekday.

Summer ITs — Air Malta B720/B737; Aviaco DC8/DC9; B.Cal. BAC1-11; Balkan Tu1543; Dan-Air B727; Aviogenex Tu134; Britannia B737; Aeroflot Tu134/Tu154; British Midland DC9; Inex Adria DC9; LOT IL18/Tu134; JAT B727; Monarch B720; Trans Europa Caravelle; Tunis Air B737; Tarom Tu154; WDL F27; Olympic B707.

1982

27 March. British Airways 'Farewell to the Viscount' charter to Kirkwall (returning on 28th March) utilising G-AOYL/M/O and G-APIM.

2 April. Icelandair return to Glasgow — Copenhagen route.

April. British Airways, in the grip of business recession and severe financial problems, re-organise their Scottish operations forming the Highlands Division at Glasgow Airport. New, unique operating practices were introduced to make possible a reliable operation and safeguard the long-established Scottish operations.

8 May. Last Viscount schedule — BA572I, Inverness — Glasgow, G-AOYM.

May. British Airways' Viscounts finally retired in Scotland, more HS748s ordered.

25 Oct. British Midland, having won their appeal, start Glasgow — Heathrow services — six flights daily, Monday to Friday; four flights on Saturday and Sunday. First southbound flight BMA001 DC9, G-BMAB.

Scandinavian Air Services ceased Glasgow — Copenhagen freighter services.

Summer ITs — Aviaco DC8/DC9; Balair DC9; Spantax CV990/DC8; Iberia DC9; Aviogenex Tu134; Inex Adria DC9; JAT B727; Air Malta B737; Balkan Tu154; Tarom Tu154; Britannia B737; Aeroflot Tu134/Tu154; TAP B707; B.Cal. BAC1-11; Dan-Air BC1-11; Monarch B737.

1983

5 Jan. B.Cal. BAC1-11 Srs 5l5, G-AZPZ, named 'City of Glasgow' at a ceremony at the airport — name previously on BAC1-11 Srs 201, G-ASJC.

8 Feb. First visit by British Airways' new Boeing 757 aircraft, G-BIKB.

11 Feb. B757 start operations on 'Shuttle'.

23 Feb. Trident 1C, G-ARPP's last flight as 'Shuttle 6F' — then to BAA fire service.

14 May. 50 years of Scottish Air Ambulance — (first flight 14th May, 1933, Islay to Glasgow in Midland and Scottish Air Ferries Ltd. DH84, Dragon piloted by J.H. Orrell).

7 June. NASA Boeing 747 N905NA with Space Shuttle 'Enterprise' performs low pass.

30 Aug. Inauguration of British Airways' 'Super Shuttle', Glasgow — London service — no less than three of their Concordes were together at Glasgow in celebration. G-BOAD with Sir Colin Marshall, and G-BOAA and G-BOAB.

22 October. Opening, by Marshal of the Royal Air Force, Lord Cameron, of the 602 (City of Glasgow) Squadron Museum adjacent to 2175 (Rolls Royce) Squadron Air Training Corps. headquarters at Hillington.

Summer ITs — Aviaco B727/DC8?DC9; Aviogenex Tu134; JAT DC9; Inex Adria DC9; Air Malta B720/B737; Balkan Tu134/Tu154; B.Cal. DC10 (first regular wide-bodied operation); Orion B737; Britannia B737; Spantax DC8; British Island BAC1-11; LOT IL18; Tunis Air B737.

Winter ITs 1983/84 — Aviaco B727/DC9; Britannia B737; Swissair DC9.

1984

21 March. First visit of type — A310, G-BKWU, British Caledonian.

26 March. Metropolitan takeover from Dan-Air on Leeds — Bradford route, then start a Newcastle route in association with B.Cal.

End March. Burnthills suspend helicopter services — restarted limited services to Rothesay, mid August.

1 May. First regular B747 service to Glasgow started by Aviaco using Iberia aircraft from/to Tenerife — first movement EC-DIA.

25 Sept. Loganair start Glasgow — Manchester services.

1 Oct. Air Uk takeover British Caledonian's Glasgow — Newcastle — Amsterdam services initially using British Island BAC1-11s until deliver of leased Fokker F28.

18 Oct. British Airtours B747, G-BDXL diverted from Prestwick due to crosswinds, then routed direct to Toronto.

13 Dec. Delivery of HS748/2B Super, G-HDBA to British Airways Highlands Division.

Summer ITs — Aviaco A300/B727/B747?DC9; Cyprus B707; Aviogenex B727/Tu134; Swissair DC9; Orion B737; Aeroflot Tu134/Tu154; TAP B727; Inex Adria DC9; B.Ca. DC10; Tunis Air B737; Hispania Caravelle; British Airtours B737; Spantax DC8/DC9; Dan-Air BAC1-11; Balkan Tu154; LOT IL18; Monarch B737/B757; Britannia B737; British Airways TriStar.

Winter ITs — 1984/85 — Aviaco B747/DC9; Cyprus B707; TAP B737; Hispania Caravelle; Dan-Air BAC1-11; Inex Adria DC9; British Island BAC1-11; Britannia B737.

May. The Leeds/Bradford service was taken over by Brown Air in May and Malinair ceased operations on 19 June. Swissair introduced an A.310 freight service Zurich — Glasgow — Manchester — Zurich on 2 November using Airbus HB-IPH on the first flight. The first visit of an RAF Tornado F.3 was on 14 December when ZE205'AA' from 229 OCU provided the backdrop for the launch of the book "Glasgow's Own" — a history of 602 Squadron.

Air 2000 launched its Glasgow operations on 16 March 1988 with Boeing 757 G-OOOC featuring in a 'laser extravaganza' while Air France began a Paris — Glasgow — Aberdeen — Glasgow — Paris service six days a week on 27 March with Boeing 737s or F.28s nightstopping at Aberden — first flight by B.737 F-GFLV. The same month KLM's Amsterdam services were transferred to Air UK and that airline also began a Stansted- Glasgow service with Fokker F.27s. On 25 April Ryanair introduced a BAC 1-11 service to Dublin with EI-BVH but withdrew from the route on 9 September. SAS extended its service to Dublin on 27 June six days a week and November saw Air UK taking over the BA/BCal Gatwick services from Glasgow and Edinburgh. Scottish European Airways started services to Brussels and Frankfurt on 14 November using ex-Chieftain HS.748s (re-registered G-BPDA & G-BPFU) and the first BAe.ATP for BA Highlands Division, G-BTPA 'Strathallan', was delivered on 22 December.

On 1 February 1989 Sabena introduced a Brussels — Manchester — Glasgow service with F.28 aircraft (first service by OO-DJB) although the route was subsequently changed to Brussels — Edinburgh — Glasgow — Brussels. Lufthansa upgraded the Dusseldorf service on 28 March to RFG ATR.42 aircraft (first service by D-BCRN) and on 7 May Air 2000 began its B.757 Glasgow — (Prestwick) — Bangor — Orlando service using G-OOOH — the aircraft positioned back to Glasgow direct the following day. The airline's first direct service to Glasgow from Orlando was on 14 September with a direct outbound to Bangor — Orlando on 17 September.

The change of Prestwick's 'trans-Atlantic gateway status' announced on Tuesday 6th March 1990 provided the opportunity for both British and foreign airlines to fly scheduled services from Glasgow Airport to North America. Northwest Airlines and Air Canada said they would transfer their operations to Glasgow and the arrival of flight NW34 at 0810hrs on Wednesday, 2 May heralded the introduction of regular inter-continental flights. The Northwest DC10, N149US, was in the airline's new red, white and grey livery and the outgoing flight headed west for Boston as NW35. On 16 May the first Air Canada flight, AC860 arrived from Halifax (via London) at 0946hrs, was with Boeing 767 C-GDSP and returned to Halifax at 1045hrs. On the same day American Airlines introduced its new daily service from Chicago, AA52 landing at 1029hrs, with Boeing 767 N327AA, and the outbound service to Chicago, AA53, took to the air at 1409hrs. British Airways introduced services on 3 August 1990 with TriStars flying to New York on Fridays, Saturdays and Sundays. The inaugural flight with BA's Chairman Lord King on board was flown by G-BEAK.

In 1966 the terminal building seemed large enough for the foreseeable future but, since then, it has been extended and revamped on a number of occasions. When opened, the main runway, 06/24 (redesignated 05/23 on 24 March 1981 due to magnetic variation movement), had a length of 6,720 feet but was extended to 8,720 feet (2658m) in 1973 and has proved adequate for current needs. A subsidiary runway, 10/28 used by light aircraft up to HS748 size, is 3,570 feet (1088m) long. In 1966 there were some 10 airlines operating scheduled services from the airport (British European Airways, British United, British Eagle, British Midland, Aer Lingus, Icelandair, Loftleidir, Cambrian, Loganair and Autair). By 1990, this had grown to 17 airlines (British Airways, British Midland, Air UK, Loganair, Capital Airlines, Manx Airlines, Scottish European Airways, Sabena, SAS, Aer Lingus, Lufthansa, JAT, Air France, Icelandair, Northwest, Air Canada and American) with scheduled flights to 23 destinations in the UK and 18 overseas. Charter business has expanded considerably with nearly 30 carriers flying to over 50 overseas airports. In the year 1988/89 some 3.7 million passengers were handled of which two thirds were on scheduled flights and half of them flying to London. In the same year the total aircraft movements had risen to 105 400 and over 22 000 tonnes of cargo and mail were handled.

Third-level operators which are currently based include Air Sinclair with BN-2A Islanders (G-BEEG & G-BJSA) and a PA-23 Aztec 250E (G-BBEY), Merlin Executive operating a Cessna F406 Caravan II (G-BPSV) and PLM Helicopters with a based AS355 Squirrel. Engineering facilities are provided by British Airways, Loganair, Aircraft Engineers and Cormack (Aircraft Services).

Recreational flying is provided by the West of Scotland Flying Club with three PA28 Cherokee 140s (G-ATOJ, G-ATVO, G-AVUS) and PA23 Aztec 250F (G-KEYS), the Glasgow Flying Club with two PA38 Tomahawk 112s (G-BKMK, G-BPMS), PA28 Warrior II (G-BOIG), PA28R Turbo Arrow III (G-BNVT) and PA18 Super Cub 135 (G-ROVE) and the Renfrew Flying Club with Cessna FA152 Aerobat (G-BFYN). It is worth noting that all these clubs together with the University Air Squadron carry out flying training at a busy international airport where types varying from Concorde to Piper Cubs can be seen landing! Changed days from Renfrew after the war when with considerably less traffic flying training was forbidden until 1952.

Air Traffic Control is in the hands of the Civil Aviation Authority who cover all movements within the Scottish TMA Glasgow Special Rules Zone. Runway 05/23 is equipped with Category III autoland and the airfield has primary radar facilities with secondary radar to be introduced by 1991.

It is interesting to note that with the continual growth of commercial aviation Glasgow Airport has embarked on its most ambitious expansion yet with a three year development started in 1989 costing over £52 million. This work will result in the terminal building being increased in size by 70% with improvements in all aspects of passenger handling and a new road system will provide better access. It is scheduled to be complete by the Spring of 1993 and is being supervised by V. L. Murphy, Managing Director of Scottish Airports Ltd and Glasgow Airport.

1985
27 March. First visit of type — B767, G-GKPW Britannia Airways.

29 Dec. Last Trident movement — Trident 3B, G-AWZO on Shuttle 7L.

Dec. Malinair commence operations with two BN2 Islanders on service to Carrickfinn.

Summer ITs — Aviaco A300/B727/DC9; Balair DC9; B.Cal. DC10; Spantax DC9; Cyprus A310/B707; Dan-Air BAC1-11; Inex Adria DC9; Hispana Caravelle; Aviogenex B727/Tu134; JAT B707/B727; Air Malta B737; Balkan Tu154; LOT IL18; Aeroflot Tu134/Tu154; TAP B707/B727/B737/TriStar; Orion B737; Britannia B737.

1986
26 Jan. News International Ltd., opens newspaper printing plant at Kinnning Park, leading to significant increase in newspaper operations at night.

March. Importance of Glasgow for deliveries — four Venezuelan Navy CASA 212s, 17th-21st, five Mexican Navy CASA 212s, 22nd-24th.

1 April. Lufthansa start Dusseldorf — Glasgow services utilising DLT, EMB120 — first service F27 PT-SIH.

20 May. Icelandair resume Reykjavik — Vagar (Faroes) — Glasgow service after some 16 years — first service F27, TF-FLN.

24 Oct. Malinair took delivery of Do228 PH-SDO until first of its own (G-CFIN) arrived.

Summer ITs — Aviaco A300/B727/DC9; Balair DC9; B.Cal. DC10; Spantax B737/DC8; Cyprus A310/B707; Dan-Air B727; JAT B707; Hispania B737/Caravelle; Aviogenex B727/Tu134; Adria DC9; British Island BAC1-11; Air Malta B720/B737; LOT IL18; Balkan Tu134/Tu154; Aeroflot Tu134/Tu154; TAP B707/B727/B737; Air Charter B737; Britannia B737/DC8(!); British Midland DC9.

Winter ITs 1986/87 — Aviaco A300/B727/DC9; Cyprus A310/B707; TAP B727; Britannia B737/B767; JAT B727/B737.

1987
19 Jan. Air Ecosse suspended operations.
21 Jan. Malinair took delivery of G-CFIN while PH-SDO became G-MLDO.

March. Chieftain Airways took delivery of HS748 , G-GLAS 'The Lord Provost of Glasgow' on 5th and G-EDIN 'The Lord Provost of Edinburgh' on 20th for services to Brussels, and Be200, G-BHVX on 27th for services to Hamburg. Services launched 29th March — into receivership 13th May.

Brown Air took over Leeds — Bradford service.

4 June. BeA36 Bonanza N6757Y crashed south west of Howood, six miles from airport, while inbound from Reykjavik. Two fatalities.

19 June. Malinair ceased operations.

2 Nov. Swissair introduce A310 on Zurich — Glasgow — Manchester — Zurich freight service — first service HB-IPH.

14 Dec. First visit of type — ZE205 'AA' Tornado F3 229 OCU (for the launch of a certain book!) — 'Glasgow's Own', History of 602 (City of Glasgow) Squadron.

1988

16 Mar. Air 2000 launch Glasgow services with a 'laser extravaganza' utilising B757, G-OOOC.

27 Mar. Air France begin Paris — Glasgow — Aberdeen — Glasgow — Paris service inbound, Sun. — Fri. p.m., outbound Mon. — Sat. a.m., nightstopping in Aberdeen using B737/F28 aircraft — first service B737, F-GFLV.

KLM's Glasgow — Amsterdam services transferred to Air UK.

28 Mar. Air UK begin a Stansted — Glasgow F27 service.

25 April. Ryanair begin Dublin — Glasgow BAC1-11 service — first service EI-BVH — but route only maintained till 9th September.

27 June. SAS extend six services (excl. Saturday) through to Dublin (i.e. now third airline on Glasgow — Dublin).

Nov. Air UK takeover BA/B.Cal., Gatwick — Glasgow/Edinburgh services.

14 Nov. Scottish European Airways start Glasgow — Brussels — Glasgow — Frankfurt — Brussels — Glasgow services on weekdays utilising HS748s, G-BPDA, (ex G-GLAS) and G-BPFU (ex G-EDIN).

22 Dec. British Airways' first ATP, G-BTPA delivered to British Airways Highlands Division.

1989
1 Feb. Sabena start Brussels — Manchester — Glasgow service using F28 aircraft — first service OO-DJB — service now Brussels — Edinburgh — Glasgow — Brussels.

28 Mar. Lufthansa upgrade Dusseldorf — Glasgow service to RFG, ATR42 — first service D-BCRN.

7 May. Air 2000 start Glasgow — (Prestwick) — Bangor — Orlando service — first service, G-OOOH. Aircraft positioned directly back from Orlando next day.

14 Sept. First direct Air 2000 Orlando — Glasgow service. Boeing 757, G-OOOC.

17 Sept. First direct Air 2000 service to Bangor — Orlando. Boeing 757, G-OOOG.

13 Dec. First visit (diversion) by British Airways Boeing 747-400. G-BNLC.

1990
27 April. Scottish European Airways ceased operations.

2 May. Northwest Airlines transferred their trans-Atlantic services from Prestwick to Glasgow. First service by DC-10 series 40, N149US.

16 May. American Airlines began operations on Chicago to Glasgow route. Inaugural service was Boeing 767-223ER, N327AA.

Air Canada transfer from Prestwick to Glasgow. First service to Halifax by Boeing 767-233 ER, C-GDSP.

18 May. Air Canada's first service to Toronto from Glasgow in a Tri-Star.

3 Aug. Inaugural British Airways service. Glasgow to New York using Lockheed Tri-Star G-BEAK.

A history of this nature would not be complete without some reference to the operations of Loganair. Its origins are found in Capital Services (Aero) Ltd in 1961 with Captain Duncan McIntosh as Chief Pilot but Loganair itself was formed on 1 February 1962 as the aviation division of the Logan Construction Co Ltd. with the first two aircraft being a Piper PA23 Aztec (G-ARMH) and a Piper PA22 Tri-Pacer (G-ARHV). In 1963 a further Aztec and a Cherokee 180 were added to the fleet and the first scheduled service between Dundee and Edinburgh commenced in October. Sadly, Willie Logan, founder of the company was killed in an air accident on 23 January 1966 but the business continued and grew, moving to the new Glasgow Airport at Abbotsinch on 2 May that year. Scheduled services continued to expand and the first Britten-Norman Islander was delivered in 1967. Air Ambulance flights also commenced that year but 1968 saw the arrival of the Beech E18s which later operated on the company's international route from Glasgow and Aberdeen to Stavanger. Loganair Ltd was acquired by the National Commercial Bank of Scotland in October 1968 which merged with the Royal Bank of Scotland the following year. In 1973 the company was awarded the full Air Ambulance service. Captain McIntosh retired in 1982 after 21 years service and Scott Grier took over as Managing Director. In December 1983 Loganair became part of the Airlines of Britain Group but has retained its individual identity. As Scotland's Airline Loganair can lay claim to a number of records like operating the world's shortest scheduled flight between the Orcadian islands of Westray and Papa Westray with a timetabled duration of two minutes — it has been done in 58 seconds! It was the world's largest Trilander operator and currently flies to more destinations in the UK than any other airline.

Development of the helicopter for commercial operators was most marked in the 1950s and 60s with an increase in use seen in many areas. A city centre heli-pad was created on the stone base of an old crane at Finnieston Street adjacent to the River Clyde and this was used until the present site at the Scottish Exhibition Centre was opened in 1988. Helicopters are now a familiar sight in our skies but best known is the Radio Clyde's Jet Ranger with Captain George Muir giving traffic reports. Strathclyde Police have recently taken to the air with the introduction of a Bolkow 105D G-BFYA offering greater mobility.

By August 1990, the first trans-Atlantic carriers had established themselves at Glasgow Airport offering direct flights to New York, Boston, Chicago, Halifax and Toronto. As a result the airport is much busier and a temporary check-in terminal has been provided to cater for these services pending the completion of the present building programme which will greatly improve facilities for both airlines and their passengers.

And what of the future? The management are currently looking at further expansion to cope with projected traffic increase and keep Glasgow as a major international airport. British Airways has also announced its plans for moving the maintenance of the One-Eleven fleet from Birmingham and Manchester to Glasgow. The trees may still remain at Arkleston but those seventy years have seen a mightly leap in aviation in the West of Scotland.

Air '2000', the airline that forced the issue of transatlantic gateway status for Abbotsinch. Seen here is one of their Boeing 757s, G-OOOJ, May 1990.

Northwest Airlines' inaugural flight from Boston to Glasgow, Abbotsinch, 2nd May 1990, DC-10 Series 40, N149 US.

One of Prestwick's oldest customers, Air Canada, formerly Trans Canada Airlines, transferred their services to Abbotsinch on 16th May 1990. Their first flight out was to Halifax with Boeing 767, C-GDSP. Note the daily Air Bridge Vanguard in the background.

American Airlines inaugurated their Chicago to Glasgow service on 16th May 1990, with Boeing 767, N327 AA. The short-lived associated company, American Overseas Airlines had operated to Prestwick during the late 1940s.

Inaugural British Airways service from Glasgow Airport to New York on 3rd August 1990. Lockheed Tri-star-50, G-BEAK. A BA Boeing 757 on the Super Shuttle service to London is in the background.

These illustrations show artists' impressions of the exterior and interior of the new Glasgow Airport terminal due to be completed in 1993.

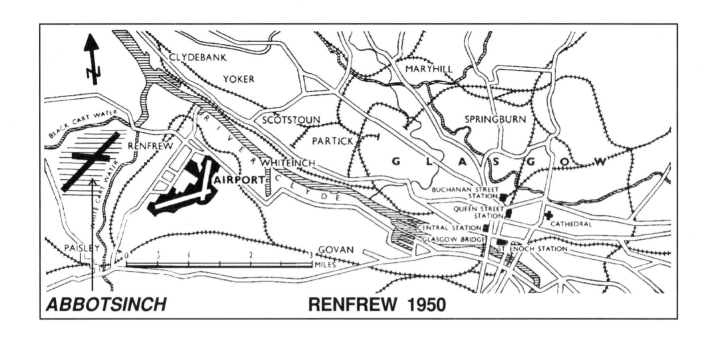

ABBOTSINCH **RENFREW 1950**

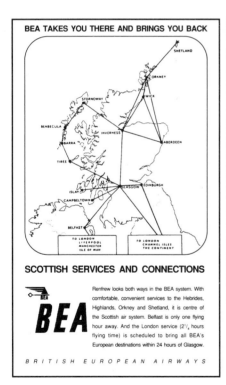

BEA TAKES YOU THERE AND BRINGS YOU BACK

SCOTTISH SERVICES AND CONNECTIONS

Renfrew looks both ways in the BEA system. With comfortable, convenient services to the Hebrides, Highlands, Orkney and Shetland, it is centre of the Scottish air system. Belfast is only one flying hour away. And the London service (2¹/₄ hours flying time) is scheduled to bring all BEA's European destinations within 24 hours of Glasgow.

BRITISH EUROPEAN AIRWAYS

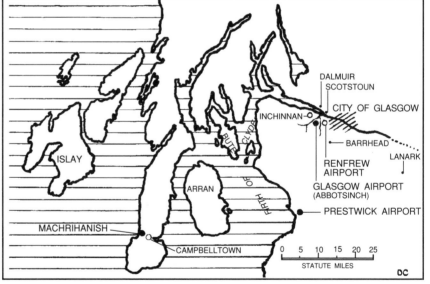